Advance Praise

"Jack Murray is a great storyteller, but more importantly he is a wonderful teacher. *The Magic Slice* is a thought-provoking process that will help you to shape your stories."

Will McInnes, former CMO of Brandwatch and author of *Culture Shock*

"Do you want to find that place (the Magic Slice) where the story you have to tell meets your customers' challenge? Then this book is for you. Jack has created an extremely practical guide that will help supercharge your creativity and storytelling."

Brian Storm, Founder of Mediastorm

"I was gripped from the first page. Jack Murray reveals the science, creative spark, and know-how that you need to master to become a great storyteller. *The Magic Slice* is a must for anyone who wants to be a better communicator."

Louise Foody, Director of Digital and Brand at Kingspan

"Jack Murray is a natural storyteller. I can say this with authority as I have personally observed the effect his workshops and presentations have had on lottery managers from every country in Europe over the past ten years. He brings his unique skill—not to mention his extensive experience— to bear on this book, which is full of personal experiences, checklists, practical examples, and exercises—a comprehensive communications cookbook. If you want to be a better storyteller, quite simply, you need to read this book."

Ray Bates, Honorary President of European Lotteries

"This is a great book that demystifies the art of storytelling and unveils a simple process that anyone can follow to be a skilled communicator."

Pat Phelan, Co-Founder of Sisu Aesthetic Clinic

"Stories are the bridge to getting ideas from your mind to the minds of others. If you want to understand how to put stories at the heart of your mission, read this book. Jack blends theory, narrative, and practical know-how to give you the tools you need to tell stories."

Patrick Campbell, CEO and Founder of Profitwell.

"This book provides a road map for any individual or organization that seeks to become masterful communicators through storytelling. Jack's practical and personal knowledge are accessible to anyone."

John Collins, Head of Content & Communications at Ramp and former Director of Content at Intercom

"I've been helping keynote speakers construct narratives for over fifteen years, and I still learned something right from the book's introduction. Like any great story, Jack Murray's *The Magic Slice* is both compelling and insightful and will be a great tool for any communicator looking to up their game."

Herb Kim, Founder of the Thinking Digital Conference

"Jack is a natural storyteller who shares his insights, expertise, and processes for telling great stories in this practical, actionable, and engaging read. His 'Magic Slice' formula is a must-read for anyone trying to gain the attention of an audience."

Áine Kerr, Co-Founder and COO of Kinzen

The Magic Slice

The Magic Slice

How to Master the Art of Storytelling for Business

Jack Murray

HOUNDSTOOTH
PRESS

For my dad, who lit the story spark in me.

Contents

Great stories get more...

...attention

...emotional connection

...funding

...loyalty

...sales.

Consider this problem:

You have a great product or service, but nobody else knows about it. You are brimming with enthusiasm, but you don't know how to spread the word and get your message out.

You have a *communications* issue, but don't know where to start to solve it. You ask yourself, "What could I say to my customers that might be interesting?" And then you realize that—even if you knew the right information to share—you have no idea how to shape it the correct way to grab their attention.

You need a story.

You have a communication problem.

I have a solution in six easy steps.

Introduction

Why Storytelling Is the Only Way

This book is about how to create great stories and how to use them effectively to communicate and engage with customers and generate business.

Ever since I can remember, I've been obsessed with the craft of storytelling. It all started with a story my dad told me when I was small about the man in the picture below: my great-grandfather, John Murray. The picture was taken in the late 1800s. The woman beside him is his mother, Catherine.

Ireland was an exceptionally poor place in the 1880s, and my family had a small farm of twenty-nine acres in south Roscommon, in the middle of the country, just west of the River Shannon. John was the eldest of nine children, and times were tough. The Murrays, like many small farmers, struggled to pay the rent and put food on the table at the same time. Evictions were common; if you couldn't pay the landlord, you would be forced out of your home and off the land.

In 1886, at twenty-nine years of age, John made the most difficult decision of his life: to leave home and go to America. His only motivation was to make enough money to help his family survive.

His ship, the RMS *Aurania*, docked at Castle Garden on the southern tip of Manhattan on April 18, Palm Sunday. He disembarked, ready to have his immigration papers processed, not knowing what was ahead of him. Imagine what it was like for an innocent country man in a bustling metropolis like New York in the 1880s. It must have been mind-blowing.

Back then, the great city was overrun by criminality and corruption. It was controlled by the twin malign forces of criminal gangs and the Tammany Hall political organization. The first "skyscrapers" were just being built, and each day thousands of immigrants arrived from every corner of the globe.

The arriving Irish gravitated toward the Lower East Side of Manhattan, where they crammed into tenements with little or no sanitation. Disease was rife. Dead animals were left in the streets for weeks. If you survived the pickpockets and the gang violence, then you might have caught cholera, typhus, or tuberculosis. It wasn't a place for the fainthearted.

Our family history doesn't record precisely what Great-Grandfather John did while he was in New York or exactly how long he stayed, but we do know something remarkable happened, which resonates to this day—almost 150 years later.

During his time in New York, John got an idea to start a business. He opened a general store, a trading post for the farming community. I often imagine him walking into one of those enormous, overflowing American stores and getting the idea. It's clear he committed himself to it because, extraordinarily, a number of years later he arrived back in Ireland with enough money to set up that same business in his hometown of Ballinasloe.

Here they are on the opening day—my great-grandfather on the left, with his wife, Margaret, and three of their seven children. My great-uncle Martin is holding the donkey.

I love this picture so much. It is a defining moment in the history of our family. One man's brave decision to change the direction of his family's fortunes is still being felt today. My great-grandfather's business lives on, and today is run by my mother, Noreen, and my brother, Kevin. (If you look closely into the shop window, you can see Jameson whiskey and Oxo cubes—two more brands that still exist.)

The business is where I grew up and learned about the craft of storytelling. We have many old grain lofts, and wherever you look, you are surrounded by history and relics from the past.

When I was small, each evening after the shop closed, we would sit down for a meal and discuss the day's events. Who stopped by, what did they want, and did they have any news? My dad's contribution would often begin with the phrase "You'll never believe what I heard down the yard today." This was often followed by a wondrous tale, always part fact, part embellishment, all to keep us engaged and entertained. It's easy to see how I got hooked on stories.

I studied marketing at university before taking a postgraduate course in journalism. By that stage, I had realized I wanted storytelling to have a huge part in my life. As soon as I qualified, I began working for a political party as a press officer. My job was what is sometimes called that of a "spin doctor," trying to get the best media coverage for the candidates I worked with. I then progressed to providing strategic communications advice to CEOs before I founded MediaHQ. We're a media database, and we build software that allows people to share their stories with journalists to help make and shape the news. There is a single strand that runs through all of this: storytelling.

My dad loved to work and thrived on getting stuck into a physical job, breaking sweat, and getting dirt under his fingernails. He was a man of action and was more than a little bemused with my career in communications. When anyone asked him what I did for a living, he would pause, then grin and say:

"He's selling talk above in Dublin."

That describes my job beautifully. I realized a long time ago that storytelling was the only way to communicate. From the start of my career, the currency of success has always been the quality of the stories I had to tell. On the days I really struggled to get the world to take notice, I would think, *If only I had a better story today, life would be so much easier.* I knew if I had a better story, I would get more attention, more engagement, and more interest. The quest was always to make the story I had better, and through that drive I learned a valuable lesson.

The next time you are struggling to get the world to care about your work, remember this:

Those with the best stories succeed.

Stories Have the Power to Do the Heavy Lifting in Every Aspect of Work

Consider for a minute how stories drive success in:

- Your mission and values

- Communicating with authenticity

- Requests for funding

- Speeches and presentations

- Recruiting

- Sales and marketing

- PR, social media, and content marketing

Why, then, are people more inclined to write boring articles and create slide decks full of bullet points than they are to share emotionally charged stories? It's simple, really: it's easier. Being original, engaging, interesting, or funny takes much more effort. But it's worth it.

What Is This Book About?

This book is about storytelling, but it's not just about that. It's also about a special place called the Magic Slice, where the stories you tell resonate perfectly with your audiences and get them to act in a way that will drive your success.

No one wants to listen to everything you have to say, and really great communicators know the stories that resonate with their audiences. Look at this diagram below. This is what your Magic Slice looks like:

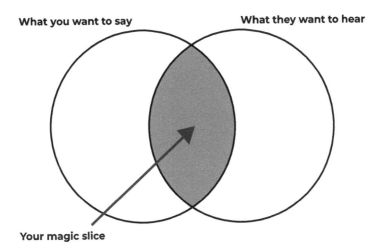

What you want to say

What they want to hear

Your magic slice

The areas of these two circles and the contents within are never fixed; instead, they are dynamic and constantly shifting. Sometimes, on really good days when you are telling great stories, the two circles become one. An example of this would be the day NASA landed the Perseverance rover on Mars: the whole world was tuned in and wanted to hear every last detail. But it's important to recognize that days like this are rare. Often, the two circles don't touch at all and no one is interested in what you have to say.

Understanding your Magic Slice is about knowing how to tell a great story, but, more importantly, it's about how stories are constructed and told so the audience can hear them clearly every time.

The good news is that everyone can learn how to find their Magic Slice, and this book will show you how to get there consistently. All it takes is a creative spark, an understanding of how stories really work, and a small bit of craft. Then you will be communicating great stories from your Magic Slice and resonating with your audiences.

This book is for you if:

- You are a **founder or a CEO** who wants to identify the stories that will get the world to listen to your idea.

- You are an **HR director** who is tired of how everyone in your organization reads bullet points from boring slide decks and puts everyone to sleep.

- You are a **PR or communications professional** who knows how to write a press release, but you want to discover the power of a great story.

- You are a **marketing director** of an established business who needs to rediscover a spark to connect with your customers.

- You're a **head of sales** with a great product or service and industry knowledge who wants to create a buzz but who has no clue how to tell a story.

Why Does It Matter?

When you don't communicate from your Magic Slice, it leaves a distinct trail, and the signs of what went wrong will be evident if you know where to look.

1. Nobody Knows the Mission, Let Alone How to Articulate It

Here's a test for you. Think about your company. Are the most basic questions, like "Why are we doing this?" or "Why do we exist?" enough to cause you utter consternation? Do you spend too much time explaining who you are and what you do? When you don't have an easy-to-understand mission, it is almost impossible to communicate clearly about what you are trying to achieve. That puts you at a distinct competitive disadvantage.

Nothing exists in a vacuum. When you don't define who you are and why you exist, then your customers—or, worse, your competitors—will do it for you. When there is no clear mission, staff often get lost in busywork to distract themselves, and this can be costly. A few years ago, I was pitching to complete the story strategy for a large hotel chain. As my pitch progressed, I could see the hotel's operations manager getting more and more agitated. Eventually he erupted. "This is all grand about our mission, but I'm just worried about how I'm going to sell the rooms on a Tuesday night in February!" For him, the central reason why they existed was less important than an immediate, pressing problem. Does this sound familiar?

The way to discover if you have a mission problem is to talk to people. Talk to good customers and ask them why they chose you over other alternatives. Ask three of your own team members from different parts of the organization to articulate your mission; if they can't, or you get widely different answers, then you have a problem you need to fix.

2. No One Who Works for the Company Can Get the Message out Effectively

Is any *one* person in your organization responsible for communications? Maybe you have a marketing or sales manager, but no one on the team has an instinct for communications. Is it a massive stretch to complete the most basic of communications tactics, such as writing a press release or contacting a journalist? When you need to do any sort of communication, do you have to consider getting help from an outside consultant, and does the price often put you off?

3. You Don't Know Who Your Most Important Audiences Are

When you're asked who your most important audiences are, are you stumped? You may genuinely not know, or maybe you have such a broad reach, you think your audience is everybody. But when you think your audience is everybody, then you can be sure it's really nobody, because it means you are making no attempt to define to whom you are trying to communicate. Do you marvel at how well the market leader in your industry is doing and how well they are tuned in to their customers? If you feel like this, you have a serious issue that needs to be addressed. By discovering your Magic Slice, you will know exactly who your most important audiences are.

4. You Worry That You Don't Communicate Often Enough

If you look at your "latest news" section of your company website, is there about one story every six weeks? And are none of them much good? To anybody looking in from the outside, does it look like you are simply ticking a box when it comes to communication, and not terribly well? Do you tend to share dry product or service news, new appointments and company announcements that are devoid of any real news value? When you communicate like this, it is a complete waste of time and money. No one reads it. By discovering your Magic Slice, you will rediscover the instinct for communications, and you will communicate more clearly and more successfully.

5. Your Organizational Culture Places No Real Value on Creativity

Does your organization's culture value technical stuff like productivity and finance over less tangible skills, such as the generation of ideas or creativity? Do you claim to encourage new ideas but then leave no space for them to develop? It is only by making real space for creativity that you will solve this problem.

6. Presentations Are "Death by PowerPoint"

Are meetings nothing but dull PowerPoint slides read out loud in a monotonous tone bullet point after bullet point? Do you drift into a daze when one of your colleagues presents their work? Knowing your Magic Slice means you are driven by stories and know how to place them as central items in how you communicate. Presentations that are story-driven are engaging, resonant, and memorable.

Finding Your Magic Slice Is Always Worth It

The Magic Slice isn't about rules or principles. It's about finding the story strategy that works for you and delivers the results you need.

The former Irish prime minister Garret Fitzgerald was a highly learned man, a decorated academic. When a civil servant once presented him with an ingenious solution to a difficult problem, he is reported to have said:

"That's all great in practice, but how will it work in theory?"

The Magic Slice is a practical solution to your pressing communications problems. It is derived from my work of over twenty years with communications professionals in a wide range of sectors and contexts. One of my catchphrases is "If it was easy, they'd all be doing it." Finding your Magic Slice will take effort, but it's definitely worth it. Knowing your Magic Slice allows you to exploit your unique voice, one your audiences understand and want to hear. It will set you apart from your competitors and will earn valued attention that will lead to success.

Why Does the World Need Another Storytelling Book?

A good question. Storytelling has been around far longer than recorded history. It is estimated that the cave paintings at Lascaux in southwest France are over seventeen thousand years old.

People have been telling stories for a long time. By this stage you'd imagine enough has been written about the process and there is no need for another book to explain it. That's what I thought, too, until I investigated further. I realized there are plenty of books out there outlining what storytelling is and how it is used in film, theatre, writing and even business. But the books that show you how to do it for yourself, your brand, or your organization are—as my dad used to say—"rare as hens' teeth."

That's why I decided to break down my methodology based on my many years of practical use and refinement. This methodology can help you identify and articulate your own Magic Slice. I want to enable you to tell compelling stories that will ensure you consistently resonate with your audiences and get them to help you achieve your goals.

The good news is that plenty of organizations know their Magic Slice, and they know how to communicate effectively from it.

In this book, we will learn from brands and organizations that communicate with great stories from their Magic Slice. We will look at how:

- **Intercom** created a software platform for customer engagement and drove massive growth through its story strategy.

- David and Clare Hieatt created **Hiut Denim** with a story and inspired royalty and rock stars to wear their jeans.

- **Amazon** uses six-page narrative memos and press releases about planned new products to drive its growth and innovation.

- **Yvon Chouinard** created Patagonia as an ethical and mission-driven brand powered by storytelling.

- **Marriott** created a story revolution by getting its leader to embrace blogging.

How to Use This Book

This is a practical book designed to help you to find your Magic Slice and become a great storyteller. At the end of each chapter I share "Points to Ponder" to help you focus on the most important issues and the things you need to change or act upon. Each chapter also has practical exercises for you to do, and I suggest you do the exercises as you go. You should look at them like bricks in a wall: the more you add in, the stronger the wall will be.

There are three parts in this book, and for the best results, they should be followed chronologically.

Part 1—How to Unlock the Power of Storytelling

- I talk about how I discovered the Magic Slice.

- I describe what a story is and what it isn't and examine the three parts of a story:

  ○ The elements

- ○ The structure

- ○ The form

- I look at how to fuel your storytelling with creativity.

- I reveal the science behind why stories are the best way to communicate.

Part 2—The Six-Step Magic Slice Process

In Part 2, I outline the elements of the Magic Slice and chart a path for you to follow to develop it. The exercises here are essential. We go through these six steps:

- Step 1—Find a mission and articulate it.

- Step 2—Tune in to your different audiences.

- Step 3—Create your Magic Slice Topics for stories.

- Step 4—Create your Magic Slice Statement.

- Step 5—Generate compelling stories.

- Step 6—Revise and edit your stories in the light of experience and the changing environment.

Part 3—Putting Storytelling to Work for You

When you get to this section, you will know why stories are so powerful and how to tell them from your Magic Slice. We will focus on what you need to do to tell great stories and when you should tell them. In particular, we will focus on:

- **Opportunity**: how to tell a story every chance you get

- **Storytelling culture**: how you can put a story machine at the heart of your organization

- **Public speaking**: how to end terrible PowerPoints and face the crowd with stories

- **Brand newsrooms**: how to tell your story on your terms

- **Glossary of Storytelling Tools**: a look at all of the story tools you can avail of

There is no time to waste. Let's embrace storytelling together and get started on finding your Magic Slice.

1

How to Unlock the Power of Storytelling

Story = the most powerful

communications tool. A simple way to

convey intention, meaning, and emotion.

How I Discovered the Concept of the Magic Slice

In the autumn of 2015, I was busy preparing for a milestone in my day job as CEO of MediaHQ, the media contacts software company I founded. We were about to achieve something we hadn't thought was vaguely possible when I started the project nine years earlier.

I purchased the business in 2006 from decorated Irish journalist Mike Burns. The much-beloved professional had started it with his wife, Lynette Fegan, in 1991, as a printed media directory. It was a big, thick spiral-bound book.

I had a passion for contacts, and for connecting people, that I had absorbed from my late dad, Joe, who taught me you can never know enough people. His motto in business was:

"Deal with Joe—the man you know."

He was so passionate about knowing people that it struck a chord with me. By 2006, I had been practicing public relations for almost a decade and was keen to roll up my sleeves, start a business, and make something new. I took out a big bank loan to pay for my new acquisition.

I soon realized that a printed book wasn't the way to connect the world with the fast-moving, always changing modern media landscape. After a moment of panic, I decided to completely change what we did. I ditched the printed book in favor of a software product that would make it easy for PR people to find journalists and send them press releases and pitches. Our mission was simple: remove all the grunt work from PR and make it easy to make the news and share your story. I was building a story factory—the MediaHQ software was born.

Fast-forward to October 2015. We were approaching the milestone of a customer about to use MediaHQ to share the hundred thousandth story through the software. It was a big moment. We'd come a long way. In a few short years, we'd gone from dealing with printers to dealing with software developers and data scientists.

And when the moment arrived, something really strange happened: I had an epiphany, a revelation about the true nature of communications. As I reflected on the thousands of stories that had been shared using MediaHQ, a crystal-clear thought began to form. The previous seven years and one hundred thousand headlines, and the stories behind them, fused into a single thought about how stories are created and shared.

In my moment of clarity, I understood how the most successful organizations use storytelling to build their success. I realized that the most engaging organizations, entrepreneurs, charities, and causes create and share their stories in their own unique way.

For the first time, I understood there is a place where the attention of an audience perfectly aligns to the power of a story. In this place, the audience is most receptive and open to the story's power. I could see it clearly in my mind's eye. I called my insight the **Magic Slice**.

Imagine it as the intersection of two circles, where one

circle is what you want to talk about and the other is what people are interested in. Your Magic Slice is where they intersect.

The Magic Slice

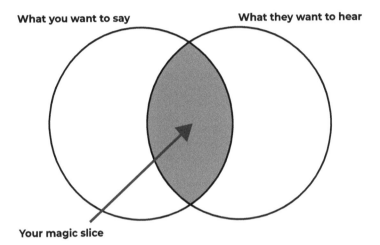

What you want to say

What they want to hear

Your magic slice

The Magic Slice is a special place where you have the undivided attention of your audience. It is a place where your stories perfectly fit what your audience is looking for. Who wouldn't want that?

I realized that an understanding of their unique Magic Slice is what makes the most successful customers of MediaHQ great at connecting their stories. A brand like Paddy Power always knows exactly who it is talking to and is always unashamedly itself. It has a personality. Or Dogs Trust, which channels its mission into every story it tells:

"To bring about the day when all dogs can enjoy a happy life, free from the threat of unnecessary destruction."

When I dug a little further, I found the power of the Magic Slice in other successful story-driven brands around the world. The Magic Slice is what makes Yvon Chouinard's story of founding the ethical adventure brand Patagonia engaging. It's what makes the story of how Hackney Council created a local newspaper the media couldn't compete with so compelling. And it's what makes David and Clare Hieatt's quest to get the small town of Cardigan in West Wales making jeans again unmissable.

In basketball terms, communicating from your Magic Slice is like nailing a three-pointer. When you communicate from your Magic Slice, you are, in essence, executing something difficult in a seemingly simple way. You tap into your mission in a way that's distinctive to you and give voice to it in the most effective way possible: a story.

When Tom Dickson, the founder of food blender company Blendtec, asks, "Will it blend?" as he stands poised to drop a phone or a golf ball into one of his machines, he is operating from the brand's Magic Slice. Blendtec's Magic Slice demonstrates the power of its blenders in YouTube videos by seeing if they can blend everyday household items. Dickson's ability to communicate from Blendtec's Magic Slice is so compelling that he became a mainstream TV star and was featured on shows like NBC's *Tonight Show with Jay Leno*.

Imagine if you could routinely, systematically, and quantifiably tell stories from your brand's Magic Slice that would resonate with your audiences. What would this look like? If your inclination is to just talk about the features of your product or service, then you are not there. Your Magic Slice is much more than that.

Your Magic Slice is where what you talk about meets the needs and excites the desires of your target audience. It's a great place to discover—the holy grail of marketing, if you like. It's about the potential of your product or service and your industry to change the world. It's about people, innovation, and creativity. And most of all, it's sewn together by compelling stories.

When you discover it, you tell stories in an engaging and interesting way. You are capturing the attention and imagination of your target audience with your unique voice.

The most successful communicators never stop searching for and refining their Magic Slice. It sets their voice and message apart from their competitors. It delivers a distinctive edge and a unique approach.

The purpose of this book is to help you to find your Magic Slice. I have developed a six-step process to help you achieve this, which we will do in the second part of this book.

Before we do that, you need to prepare to become a storyteller by understanding and acting on the answers to three questions:

- What is a story and what isn't a story?

- How do you fuel your storytelling with creativity?

- How can you be a better storyteller by understanding the science behind how stories work?

In the rest of Part 1, I have included a lot of information to help you answer these three questions.

I haven't skimped on addressing them in detail, as I know from professional experience that if answers are glossed over or not fully understood, then my six-step process loses much of its power. Not taking on board the answers to these questions will lead to the development of ineffective or, frankly, useless Magic Slices.

There is no time to delay—let's get to work.

What Is a Story—
and What Isn't a Story?

Before you start on the journey to find your Magic Slice and devise a new storytelling strategy, let's start by describing exactly what a story is.

What is a story? The most profound questions are devastatingly simple. When my two daughters were small they used to question everything. Why does the delivery person come with parcels? What is at the end of the rainbow? Where is your favorite place in the world? After being regularly on the end of this inquisition, I realized that three questions into any topic places you almost at the dawn of time.

We all instinctively know what a story is, but how do you describe it?

Let's start by saying exactly what a story isn't. I am doing this because I know you want to change how you communicate, and these "nonstories" are stopping you from succeeding.

A story isn't:

- A collection or list of random facts or events

- A spreadsheet with numbers

- A list of key performance indicators

- A technical description of a product, service, or thing

- A worthy but dull press release about something that's not terribly interesting

- A report or memo about an internal matter

- A PowerPoint presentation in the company template that's full of bullet points

Does this list look familiar? If you're looking for help to reset your story strategy and find your Magic Slice, it should resonate. The methods above are all ways of communicating that completely lack any story element or storytelling technique. Some of these methods may, of course, be necessary for work, but they all could be made much more engaging by using stories.

Back to the question at hand: What is a story? In simple terms, a story is:

An account of something that conveys meaning. It often involves people, events, and action. A story, in its simplest form, is about a character and the things that happen to them.

Everywhere you turn, there are stories. You use stories every second of every day. You constantly tell yourself stories in your head. What do you believe? What do you expect? What do you think about yourself and about other people or events that have happened? Your memories and dreams are stories; your feelings are fueled and experienced as stories. When you want someone to know you really well, you share stories about your childhood, school, family relationships, and traumas.

In this book, you will hear plenty of mentions of the individuals or groups that are on the receiving end of a story. They are called the audience. An audience can be internal to your organization, which means it can be easier to reach and influence but also easier to take for granted. Or an audience can also be external to your organization, like your customers, the media, your social media followers, or your suppliers. These audiences are harder to influence but can give the biggest positive impact. We will dive deeper into audiences as the book progresses.

The Three Parts to Telling a Good Story

We live in a golden age of storytelling. You just have to look at the story factories that are Amazon Prime, Disney, HBO, Hulu, Netflix, and Sky to realize the insatiable demand that exists for storytelling. This also means we are all exposed to many more stories than ever before. *The Sopranos* first aired in January 1999 and went on to become the first one-hundred-hour story of the modern era. We consumed it and wanted more—that is the power of storytelling.

As a result of this increased exposure to stories, audiences now have a sophisticated and innate understanding of how a story works, how they want to experience it, and what a great story looks like. They wouldn't necessarily be able to tell you how a story is working or why stories make them feel the way they do, but they definitely know what a great story feels like.

The good news is that there is an established process to create a great story, and I want to share it with you. This will help you to make sense of all that great television you have watched, but, more importantly, it will show you how to shape and execute your stories to get maximum exposure and impact.

There are three distinct parts to a story. These often get confused, which leads to a lack of clarity and poor execution. It is essential that you clearly understand each one and know how to apply them.

They are:

1. The elements of a story

2. The structure of a story

3. The form a story takes

These three parts of telling a story get confused because you will start thinking about a story in its form rather than what its key elements are or how it should be structured. People often say things like "Let's do a podcast," or "We need to do a press release," or "Why don't we do a short video?" That's understandable. It's human nature to go to the most defined thing, which is the *form* a story takes. But this is the incorrect path. A story should always start by considering the elements, then the structure, and only lastly the form.

Let's take a look at each part in detail.

The Elements of a Story

There are eight elements to a great story. It doesn't matter if it's a two-hour feature film or a twenty-second radio advert—it is possible to include all of these elements. When you are devising a story, you should be really clear about what each of these elements is. You should complete a stocktake of what you have in your story to make sure each element is present.

The more of these elements present in your story, the better it will be. The more of them that are unclear or missing, the weaker it will be. Here they are:

- Protagonist

- Antagonist

- Need

- Inciting incident

- The Journey

- Crisis

- Climax

- Resolution

= Great story!

The eight elements of a story are outlined in detail below.

PROTAGONIST

Who is your story about? It could be your product, your customer, your founder, or you. In film, it's Batman, James Bond, or Bridget Jones. In business, it's Richard Branson of Virgin, Jo Malone of Jo Malone, or Herb Kelleher of Southwest Airlines.

Over the lifetime of a project, you will tell hundreds and hundreds of stories, but no matter what the context is, you will need a protagonist in every one. If a story doesn't have a clear and easily identifiable protagonist, it will lack definition, and if it lacks definition, people will tune out. It's as simple as that. It's important that the protagonist is either a likable or a compelling character. Either will work, but they must be one or the other.

A good example of this is Ryanair, the low fares airline. Its CEO, Michael O'Leary, is not often thought of as warm and cuddly, but he's a compelling protagonist because he's extremely competitive and challenges people every time he speaks in public. If your protagonist is neither likable nor compelling, then you will have an uphill battle. Remember, your audience has limited time to spend. Their natural urge is to root for the protagonist in a story. Make it easy for them.

ANTAGONIST

Once you have introduced your protagonist, you need to be extremely clear about the problem they are trying to solve or the difficulty they are trying to surmount. What or who is the evil force the protagonist is trying to overcome? It could be apathy, or it could be your customers' pain points. In medicine, it's usually an illness.

In the case of the undergarment Spanx, the antagonist against which company founder Sara Blakely is fighting is feeling terrible in your own skin. She started the business because she wanted to create an undergarment that women would feel supremely comfortable and confident wearing. By telling her personal story—trying to feel confident in her own clothes—she brought to life the antagonist she is fighting.

In the case of electric bike company Rad Power Bikes, CEO Mike Radenbaugh created the first bike for himself because his antagonist was a long and dangerous twenty-five-kilometer (sixteen-mile) cycle to high school each day on an ordinary bike.

NEED

Once you know the protagonist and the difficult forces they are working against, you must then answer this question:

What does the protagonist want or need?

Let's try a few examples:

Sara Blakely of Spanx

Sara Blakely was sick and tired of lacking confidence when she put on her wardrobe. She wanted to create a garment that would give women back their confidence.

Mike Radenbaugh of Rad Power Bikes

Mike Radenbaugh was stressed, tired, and a little bit smelly from cycling twenty-five kilometers (sixteen miles) to and from high school each day. He wanted to create a mode of transport that was easier and safer for these distances for people who couldn't afford a car.

Michael O'Leary of Ryanair

Michael O'Leary was angry that the airline industry was dominated by a number of large carriers charging large fares. He believes air travel should cost very little and be open to everyone.

INCITING INCIDENT

This is an event that happens to our protagonist that opens their eyes, challenges them, and gets them to act. If you like watching TV dramas, you will be familiar with this. You will be introduced to the central character, you will find out what they want or need, and then something will happen to them. This is called the inciting incident. In a TV drama or documentary, this will happen within the first five minutes. What does this look like for your story? What opposition are you encountering, and what spark gets you to act? How could you apply this to your founding story?

In the story of how I founded my business, MediaHQ, the inciting incident happened one day when I got a call from a frustrated customer. I had bought a business that published a printed media directory. It was a spiral-bound book with hundreds and hundreds of journalists' contacts.

All I wanted to do was help people make the news by sharing the best and most up-to-date journalist contact details. Making money was a massive struggle because every day large organizations came to our website, bought just one copy of the book, and then photocopied the contents. It was soul-destroying.

Then one day we got a call from Paddy Power, a huge brand and a very digitally savvy business. At the end of the call, their head of communications implored me, "Will you stop publishing the book and make a digital directory? We'll be your first customer." That was the inciting incident that set us on our way. I knew if they thought it was a good idea, it would be a huge success.

What is the spark, moment, or incident that sets your story on its way?

THE JOURNEY

The inciting incident sets our protagonist on a journey of discovery. It may seem like a storytelling cliché, but "going on a journey" is an essential element of a great story. The purpose of this journey is not only to overcome the antagonist, but also for the protagonist to learn about themselves, their weaknesses, and their strengths.

There are always two things to prove on a journey. First, there is the outward progress against the forces of evil. Second, there is the inward journey of growth and development. The protagonist has something to prove. In *Jaws*, they go to kill the shark. What is your journey?

The quality of the journey is defined by:

- How we feel about the protagonist. Do we like them? Are we rooting for them to succeed? If we are, we will be more invested in the journey.

- How we identify with the protagonist's needs. Do we understand their need? Is it universal? Can we understand why they need what they do?

"You're gonna need a bigger boat."

Police Chief Martin Brody in the 1975 film *Jaws* articulates the most famous crisis point in movie history.

CRISIS

In a story, the crisis is where your journey hits a bump in the road and you are faced with a real and difficult obstacle. The question is, How do you overcome the crisis? And what does your response to the crisis say about you? Introducing the element of crisis into a story can be a real challenge to people who are used to slick corporate communications or airbrushed social media posts. There is rarely any space for a crisis in a press release unless it is directly responding to one.

From the perspective of pacing your story, the crisis should arrive halfway through. You build tension in the story to that point. The crisis is a release, and when you deal with it, you are on the homeward stretch.

In 2015, Jeni's Splendid Ice Cream had been in business for nearly thirteen years. They were well known in Ohio.[1] They had six scoop shops, supplied high-end grocery stores, and had a strong mail-order business. What set their ice cream apart was Jeni Britton Bauer's dedicated focus on quality. The small details mattered to her, no matter the cost. The brand was on the up and up. Britton Bauer even wrote a cookbook that got the brand national attention. Everything was going great, and then the crisis hit. One day the company got a call out of the blue to say that a pint of ice cream in Lincoln, Nebraska, had tested positive for listeria.

Listeria is a bacteria found in food that can cause muscle pain, fever, diarrhea, and nausea. It can be fatal to people who are elderly, immunosuppressed, already ill, or pregnant.

What would the company do? Britton Bauer moved fast. First, she closed down production and removed all product from the market. She filed paperwork with the Food and Drug Administration, and within hours some 265 tons of ice cream that had been out in the world was on its way back to the factory. The company was working against the clock because they had six hundred staff who, at that point, had nothing to do.

Eventually they found the source of the listeria. It was coming from a hairline crack in the wall behind one of the machines in the production facility. They fixed the problem. But then Britton Bauer went above and beyond to communicate to her community what the company had done to solve the issue. She published a letter on the company website detailing every step they had taken. This included taking over two hundred swabs each day for two months, over one thousand times the industry recommendation.

Today, this crisis story is part of the story of Jeni's Splendid Ice Creams. It communicates how much they care about what they do, and it doesn't define them in a negative way. They recovered and now have over thirty stores and annual sales of $40 million.

CLIMAX

This is where your story reaches a crescendo. Your protagonist has communicated their desire, and then something happens to them that sets them on a journey. Just when they think they may have solved the problem, they face a crisis they need to overcome. When they get over the crisis, they then face their final reckoning: the climax. In film and TV, this is often the fight scene at the end.

It is where Luke Skywalker faces Darth Vader. It is the final courtroom verdict or the reveal of who actually committed the murder. In your business, it could be a product launch, a new service, winning a major competition, or achieving a huge milestone. It's the scientific team that finds a vaccine or the charity that brings clean drinking water to a community. There is always an obvious and interesting climax; you just have to look for it.

RESOLUTION

This is the moral of the story where we reflect on what we learned. It is a place to pause and process what has happened and what was learned. Here you ask:

- What are the lessons of the story?

- What did you learn about the world on your journey?

- What do you know now that you didn't know at the start?

- How have you changed as a result of your journey?

- Where do you go next, taking on board what you have learned?

The Structure of a Story

All stories have a structure. You probably don't realize it, but you learned the simplest and most fundamental rule of storytelling as soon as you could talk.

Stories have a beginning, a middle, and an end.

It seems obvious, doesn't it? It's so hardwired into all of us that it is easy to forget the power of it. The classic story structure—from the great myths to Shakespeare and every movie you know and love—is told in three acts.

The three acts can simply be described as setup, confrontation, and resolution, or beginning, middle, and end. There is a turning point toward the end of the first act and the second act.

Here's how it looks:

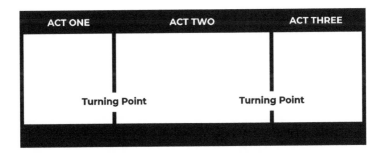

Structure lies at the heart of all modern film and television stories. I can't exaggerate how important it is to apply it. If you understand the elements of a story and how to structure it properly, then your audience will take notice (actually, if you do it well, they won't even notice they noticed). Properly constructed stories are more compelling and easier to consume and pay attention to. That's one of the main reasons you stay up far too late to binge on your favorite streamed TV series.

To make more sense of story structure, look at this diagram below. It has the elements I have outlined, mapped over the structure. You can see how the pieces fit in like a jigsaw.

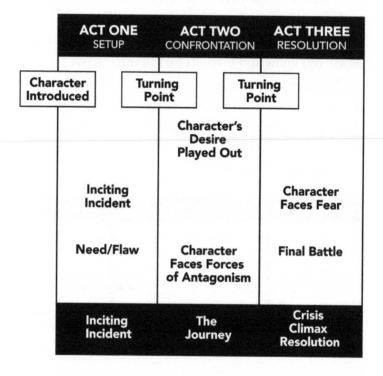

Let me give you a more detailed example of how it works in practice. I have a podcast called *Media Moments*. It started out as a program insert on a national radio station in

Ireland called Newstalk. These are brief, ten-minute stories, told over three acts, about a media moment that changed the world. The list of stories featured include the explosion of the *Challenger* space shuttle, Walter Cronkite announcing the death of JFK, and the day the novel *1984* first arrived at the publisher.

When I am preparing to write a new story about a media moment, recognizing the elements and the structure are crucial. I start by identifying the protagonist and their desire or need. The first turning point in the story is always where I reveal the media moment. That could be the moment when the aliens set "foot" on Earth in the *War of the Worlds* radio play or when Walter Cronkite announced live on television that JFK had been shot dead. To be able to write these stories, I need to know whose story it is (the protagonist), what they wanted (their need), and what the turning point was. Once I know these elements, everything else falls into place.

One other crucial factor in the structure of a story is the time you have to tell it. Time is finite and it must be respected. The *Media Moments* podcast is ten minutes. When you have a small amount of time and many things to achieve, you must be efficient. Don't forget that many of the best advertisements in the world are told in thirty seconds or less. Let's look in a bit more detail at how to plan the structure of your story by examining how an episode of the *Media Moments* podcast was planned.

THE STORY STRUCTURE OF HOW GEORGE ORWELL WROTE *1984*

I have long been fascinated by George Orwell's dystopian novel *1984*, and when I was commissioned to write and perform the *Media Moments* podcast, the story behind how the novel came to be written and published was at the top of my list. So let's look at how I structured it. The first question I asked was:

Whose Story Is This?

It could, for example, have been that of the book itself, or of the publisher, Fredric Warburg. But I decided that I was going to tell the story of George Orwell, its author, whose real name was Eric Blair.

The next question was:

What Did Eric Blair Want or Need?

When I researched his story, I discovered his motivation. It was 1944, and Blair was exhausted as World War II seemed to be nearing a conclusion. He and his wife, Eileen, longed to leave London, which had been heavily bombed. They wanted to start a family. Eric had an idea for a book he wanted to pursue and wanted to get a clean break from the oppression of wartime London. Around this time, they also adopted a boy and named him Richard. Eric got a job working for the *Observer* newspaper covering the war. But while he was away on the Continent, Eileen died suddenly during a "routine" hysterectomy. In an instant, Eric was a grief-stricken widower and a lone parent. In response, he threw himself into work. This backdrop might help to explain why *1984* is so dark. His editor at the *Observer*, David Astor, offered him his house on the remote Scottish island of Jura to write, and Eric, perhaps surprisingly, thought it was a good idea. He left with his sister Avril and infant Richard to write.

What Was the First Turning Point in the Story?

To deliver pacing and clarity to the story, it's important to find the first turning point. I always try to do this before I start to write. The podcast is called *Media Moments*, so I always make the media moment the big turning point in the story.

So what is the media moment in this story? The novel, *1984*, is such an iconic piece of culture—how do you identify just one moment? Starting out, I had no clue who the publisher was, but I wondered if it was a major event when the publisher read the manuscript for the first time. I thought he would have been the first person to validate this amazing novel. In my research, I discovered that the publisher, Fredric Warburg, had written an autobiography in which he revealed this moment and shared the notes he had written on the first manuscript. It was then that I decided the arrival by post of the first draft of the manuscript would be the media moment and the first turning point. I had no idea what address the manuscript had arrived at, but with a little search on the internet I found the sleeve of a first edition and got the office address. I then took a "virtual" stroll down the street on Google Maps like the postal delivery person did in 1948, and I was ready to tell the story. Let's look at what these elements look like in the story structure.

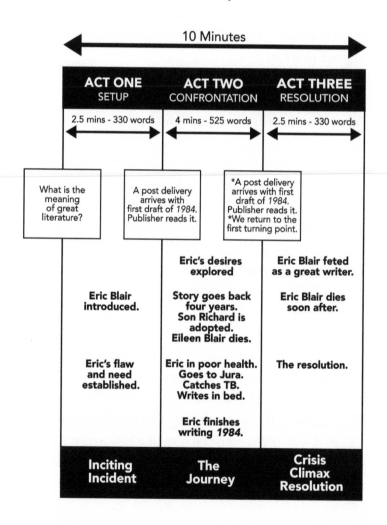

Most people just write a story and hope it works out. Storytellers know the elements and the structure; they *plan* these, and then they write the story. You can see in the *1984* example the planning and care that goes into telling a ten-minute radio story. You will notice the same turning point is visited twice in the story, which gives a real symmetry to the structure. You can apply these rules to any story you are telling. It doesn't matter if it's a keynote presentation at a conference or an example you want to use in a radio interview—if you know the elements and the structure, it will be a better story.

The Form a Story Takes

As I said at the beginning, everybody usually starts with the form a story takes, and you know by now that's the wrong place to start. You first need to know what the elements of a story are and how it is structured before you choose a form.

Every story starts in written word. Your first step as a storyteller should be to understand that and learn how to master the steps I have explained so far. Ask yourself these questions before you decide on the form a story should take:

- Do I know the elements of my story?

- Do I know how to structure my story for the best effect?

Once you have these two big decisions made, then you can start to think about the form of your story. The great thing about storytelling is there are so many and varied ways to tell a story.

It is important to be aware of and to understand the different story forms. This can get a little complicated, as there is an art to mastering each of the different forms. You can opt to master one of these forms yourself, work with a specialist in your organization, or get an outside third party to help you structure your story.

In the third part of this book, we will examine some of these story forms in detail and how you can use them every day to tell stories. For now, let's take a quick look at the form your story might take. Here are some different types of story forms:

- **A press release**: an official announcement of news by an organization in a set one- to two-page format.

- **A pitch email**: an email to a journalist pitching a story you would like them to cover. It should be creative, with a compelling story idea at its heart.

- **Website copy**: the text on a website page. It could be a product description, a founding story, a user testimonial, or a case study.

- **A blog post**: a post on an organization's website in the news or blog section. It can be opinion-, thought leadership-, review-, or experience-based. It is generally personal in nature and warm in style.

- **A media interview**: a one-on-one discussion with a journalist about a newsworthy story. It can be for radio, TV, online, or print.

- **A short film or video**: a recording normally no longer than five minutes.

- **A presentation or a speech**: a talk delivered to an audience, either with or without the aid of slides.

- **A piece of marketing collateral**: usually something physical. It could be a product, a package, or a message in a card, or some other design-written format.

- **An event or live "experience"**: an event such as a mini drama, a reading, or a story performance for an audience.

- **A podcast episode or series**: an interview or a story told by a narrator with sound clips.

- **A social media post**: a piece of content, usually text with an image or a video, posted on a social media network.

Points to Ponder

- You need to understand exactly what a story is and its place as a communications tool.

A story is an account of something that conveys meaning. It often involves people, events, and action. A story, in its simplest form, is about a character and the things that happen to them.

- There are three distinct aspects to a story. You need to know each in detail. They are:

  o The story elements: the distinct items that make a great story

  o The story structure: how a story is shaped

  o The story form: the physical form a story takes

Exercise for You

This exercise is about writing a foundation story for your organization, your brand, or yourself. A foundation story is about how it all started.

- I want you to think of a foundation story that is important to you. It could be how your organization was formed, how you got your startup idea, or how you got the big break in your career.

- Identify the different elements in the story. If an element is missing, can you find it? By adding a new element, you will improve a story that you know very well.

- Now decide how you are going to structure this story. Lay it out with notes over three acts, like in the diagram used in this chapter. Remember, the protagonist's desire, the inciting incident, and any crises all play important roles.

- Now it's time to write this story in no more than one thousand words. Keep to the limit. Structure is important, and less is always more.

Why Lighting a Creative Spark Will Fuel Your Storytelling

Everything Starts with an Idea

The first part is knowing what a story is and how to use it. The second part is understanding how to nurture your storytelling with creativity, because creativity is the fuel of storytelling.

Behind every good story is a creative storyteller, one who understands the power storytelling can have on their audience. To find your Magic Slice, you need to nurture your creativity.

Have you ever wondered what it takes to be creative? Or how you could be more creative? And is creativity something you're born with, or can you learn it?

Every book, album, app, film, and new business starts as an idea in someone's head. But the idea behind something great is different. Why? Because someone had the courage to take it on and to see it through to the end. That's the alchemy of creativity. It has a special power to turn something ordinary into something that changes people's lives.

As a young boy, I loved to create things. We always had crayons and paints in our cupboard. But there was one problem: I wasn't very good at creating. At least that was the signal I kept getting from my teachers. When I got to university, I decided to study business, but my creative itch just wouldn't go away. I kept getting an urge to write. It started as a soft, nagging voice in my head, and by the time I got to fourth year in university, it was loud and clear and telling me daily, "You need to write." Then one day, I saw an advertisement for a postgraduate course in journalism and I knew I had to apply. I found my creative outlet. The day I started the course, I instantly knew I was in the right room. I was twenty-four years old. It had taken me only sixteen years to find my creative path.

To be a storyteller, you need to generate ideas. What is standing in your way?

What Makes a Creative Person Different?

Since 2008, I have trained thousands of people to be better storytellers. I have always been intrigued by how difficult it is for people to be creative at work.

When I host a new course, my first question is "Why are you here today?" What would you guess is the most common response? It is because they don't communicate often enough. Everything in life is much more difficult if you don't do enough of it because you don't develop an instinct for it.

Many of these people just send out three or four press releases a year, and they expect, like magic, to be good at it. By the time they come to me for help, they are stuck, sometimes frozen, and often afraid to act. What is the cause of their problem? In most cases, it boils down to a lack of creativity.

Many of them work in highly corporate or serious business environments. Imagine a place that is the exact opposite of creative: an accountancy, legal, or taxation practice. These places have rules, regulations, and codes of practice, and creative thinking isn't valued. Indeed, it can be discouraged.

What is the difference between those who *struggle* to be creative and those who *succeed*? In his book on creativity, *Hegarty on Creativity: There Are No Rules*, the world-renowned advertising creative John Hegarty[2] outlines what makes creative people different from others. A colleague one day asked him a seemingly simple question:

> "What quality have you that enables you to earn a living as a creative person? In essence, what makes you different from someone who can't do that?"

Hegarty pondered a moment before realizing there was only one quality that made his creative work possible and even successful:

FEARLESSNESS

Fearlessness is the quality that is missing in many workplaces, and until you introduce it, the quality of your creativity will suffer. Think of any successful creative person you know—maybe a writer, a musician, or a painter. The fear of someone not liking their work doesn't stop them from creating. They know they simply have to keep working, producing, and acting on their ideas to get better. Creativity is consistently producing work regardless of what the world thinks.

We all have so much to learn about applying a level of fearlessness to our work. Many of the people who have sought my help on how to communicate did so because they were afraid. In the corporate world, making a bold decision or trying out a new idea is often frowned upon. Why? Because it might fail.

The organizations that succeed at communicating place a much higher value on it. This attitude is often led from the top and becomes part of a company culture—almost a natural instinct that the organization possesses. It's a paradox, but in order to succeed, you need to be willing to fail. Are you ready to challenge yourself or your organization's culture if this is impeding your creativity?

"Telling people how to be creative is easy; it's only being it that's difficult."

John Cleese on creativity

Finding Your Creative Operating System

On January 23, 1991, English comic actor John Cleese took to the stage in the Grosvenor House hotel in London to address a conference entitled Creativity in Management.[3] He began by engaging the audience with his purpose. "You know, when Video Arts asked me if I'd like to talk about creativity I said 'No problem. No problem.' Because telling people how to be creative is easy; it's only being it that's difficult."

To prepare for the talk, he said, he'd spent months poring over all of the available academic research on what makes us creative, but he came to a depressing realization: there was no evidence to explain creativity. "The reason why it is futile for me to talk about creativity is that it simply cannot be explained; it's like Mozart's music or Van Gogh's painting or Saddam Hussein's propaganda. It is literally inexplicable."[4]

Cleese said that while preparing for the talk, he came to the view that most of the research on creativity had stopped in the 1970s because people had discovered most of what they feasibly could. He then paused before revealing the golden nugget of information: "However, there is one negative thing that I can say, and it's negative because it is easier to say what creativity isn't.

"Creativity is not a talent…It is a way of operating."[5]

The first time I heard John Cleese say this, it made my head spin. "A way of operating" means creativity is not a talent or an ability that you have or don't have. It is something you can *practice*.

This is not what we're taught in school. We all believe there are certain people who are creative, and then there are those who aren't. But this is not the case.

Cleese pointed out that all of the research shows creativity is not based on your IQ. The most creative people—writers, musicians, sculptors, actors—have a process or, as Cleese described it, a "way of operating" that allows them to get into a mindset in which they can create.

He described this mindset as an ability to play, which means to explore ideas for enjoyment and not for an immediate practical purpose. Think of it like a band just jamming or an artist doodling.

Picture someone you know who's creative in the conventional sense—maybe a writer, a singer, or a designer. You will associate a specific place or method with how they create. My friend Paul is a singer and songwriter. He has a specific room where he goes to write and compose. It's in a music facility, and he is clustered with other creative people. Painters and sculptors also have studio spaces where they create.

This creativity is in a way of operating—it's not a talent that proves we all need to invest in our creative processes to get better results. We need to park the old, wrongheaded way of thinking you are either creative or you aren't.

Let's explore how to find your creative "way of operating."

The next best thing to a fully formed answer is the question that will lead you there.

Unlocking Creativity with the Power of Questions

Ever since I can remember, I have been curious, always asking questions. Curiosity is a need, an urge to find things out, to get to the end of the puzzle to solve the crime, to gain extra insight, and to understand the problem at a deeper level.

The next best thing to a fully formed answer is the question that will lead you there. The right questions have the power to open people's minds and unlock their creativity.

It was curiosity that led Sugata Mitra[6] on a journey to discover the secrets about the power of questions. Mitra taught computer programming to the children of rich parents in a school in New Delhi. Beside his school was a slum. He often wondered how it would ever be possible for the children in the slum to reach their potential. How could they learn how to program?

So he took an unusual step. He put a hole in the boundary wall of his office and put in a computer facing the slum. He wanted to see how children who didn't know what the internet was or how to read English would react. As he installed the computer, the children were curious. They asked him what it was. He said he didn't know, and when they asked if they could touch it, he said, "If you wish," and then he left.

Just eight hours later, he found them browsing and teaching themselves how to browse. He couldn't figure out how, with no previous knowledge at all, they had figured this out. Someone suggested that maybe one of his students had shown them. Now his curiosity was really piqued. He decided to take the computer-in-the-wall experiment further and, in fact, farther.

He went to a remote village three hundred miles outside of New Delhi. He knew there would be no computer engineering students passing by to help, and he wondered how the children there would react. He installed the computer and then disappeared for a few months.

When he came back, the children approached and said they wanted a faster computer and a better mouse. He asked how on earth they knew what these things were. The children got a little irritated and said, "You've given us a computer that only works in English, so we had to teach ourselves English in order to use it."

He knew something fascinating was happening. That was the first time he had heard the phrase "teach ourselves" used so casually. He started publishing his results in academic journals. His main finding was that in nine months, a group of children left alone with a computer in any language will reach the same standard and ability as an office secretary in the West.

But he wasn't finished. He was still curious about the power of what he'd discovered and wondered how far it could go. He decided to dive deeper into what he had already discovered by testing a seemingly ridiculous hypothesis.

Tamil is a language spoken in southern India, and he went to the region to test the following question:

> "Can Tamil-speaking 12-year-olds learn the biotechnology of DNA replication in English by themselves from a streetside computer?" [7]

It sounds completely crazy, doesn't it? He would test them at the start, when they would score a zero. Then he would leave them with a computer for a number of months and return to test them again, when, he presumed, they would get another zero. He would then return to the lab and say, "We need teachers."

Then he went to the village Kalikuppam. He installed computers in a wall. He downloaded educational material from the internet about the subject of DNA replication, much of which he didn't understand himself.

When the computers were turned on, the children rushed over and asked him what all the information was. He told them it was about a very topical subject, but it was all in English. They asked how they were expected to understand it. He shrugged his shoulders and gave them no help. Before he left, he tested them, and they all scored a zero.

He returned two months later. The children came to meet him and said they had understood nothing. He wasn't surprised. But he was curious to know more. He asked them how long it had taken them before they decided they hadn't understood anything. He was surprised by their response. The children said they hadn't given up and that they looked at it every single day. He asked them why they stared at the screen every day when they understood nothing. A little girl put up her hand and said:

"Well apart from the fact that improper replication of the DNA molecule causes disease, we haven't understood anything else."[8]

He tested them and got an amazing result. Their scores had gone from zero to an average of 30 percent in just two months. This was in the tropical heat with computers under a tree in a language they didn't know, and the children were doing something that was a decade ahead of their time. Amazing. But following the norms set in education, 30 percent is still a fail in an exam. Mitra wasn't satisfied and knew there was still more to his project.

He wanted to try to help them pass. He found a twenty-two-year-old local girl who worked as an accountant and who often played with the children. He asked if she would help. She said she had no knowledge of science and would be of little use. He had a different idea. He asked her to use the method of the grandmother. "What's that?" she asked. He said, "Stand behind them and whenever they do anything just say, 'Wow, how did you do that? Gosh, when I was your age, I could never have done that.'"[9]

She did that for two more months, and their scores jumped to 50 percent. Kalikuppam had caught up with his school in New Delhi, a rich private school with a bio-technology teacher.

So what did he learn from his research? He discovered the education of the future is not about rote learning and spoon-feeding students. He discovered that true learning is a by-product of educational self-organization. Education is not about making learning happen; it's about *letting* it happen. Modern education is when a teacher sets the process in motion, stands back in awe, and watches the learning happen. Mitra calls it SOLE: Self-Organised Learning Environment.

What is the role of the teacher in this new process? It is to set really big questions. Big questions pique curiosity and set people on a journey of discovery. Big questions spark the brain to life and get people into problem-solving mode. Big questions get people to work in teams, to collaborate.

What is the lesson in all of this? I think it shows clearly that to drive creativity, innovation, and learning, you need to focus on the big questions you and your colleagues should be answering. It also shows the power of great questions to unlock creativity.

Sugata Mitra's work also provides a roadmap for how to use questions to spark creativity in any group. If you are organizing a creative meeting or workshop, you should spend time beforehand designing questions that will unlock people and get them focused on the issues that matter. I always start any creative workshop with a simple "why" question that gets to the heart of the problem we are trying to solve.

- Why do our customers love X?

or

- Why do our customers do X?

The second question is usually a "what" question related to the "why" question we have just asked. So for this example, I would ask:

- What can we do to make them love X more?

The last question I ask uses the answers to the first two questions as a springboard.

- Based on everyone's answers to the first two questions, how can we make X better?

The next time you are working on a story or a project that needs fresh thinking, use these techniques. Focus on quality questions and you will unlock creativity.

Flow: a state in which people are so involved in an activity that nothing else seems to matter; the experience is so enjoyable that people will continue to do it, even at great cost, for the sheer sake of doing it.

Achieving a State of Flow— the Holy Grail of Creativity

If you have come this far in the chapter, I'm assuming you are now ready to invest in improving your creativity. You want to use it to drive your storytelling, discover your Magic Slice, and transform how you communicate.

To get this far, you have made some decisions:

- You have accepted the need to embrace creativity, both personally and where you work.

- You clearly see creativity as a way of operating and not just as a thing.

- You have opened up to the power of possibility.

- You understand the importance of resourcing your creativity.

- You are willing to take risks and realize that what you create might not be good, and that's okay.

- You know and welcome the power of questions.

All of these are powerful realizations that will change how you work and how you create. It's time to think about how you can get maximum return from the time you invest in your creativity.

The holy grail here is to achieve a mental state that is

known as *flow*. What does flow look like? When you are in a state of flow, you are completely present and fully immersed in a task. You as a creator and the universe become one, all outside distractions vanish, and your mind becomes fully open to the act of creation.

In a sense, getting to flow is like reaching a creative Nirvana. Once there, you can't be distracted and can produce high-quality work at ease. In sport, they call it being "in the zone." Imagine the mental state of a professional kicker in a field sport going through their routine before a crucial kick. They block out the world and focus intensively on the job at hand. They have a mental and physical process to get themselves into a flow state.

Mihaly Csikszentmihalyi[10] is considered one of the co-founders of positive psychology, and he was the first to identify and research flow. His research identified the eight key characteristics of achieving a flow state. They are:

1. Complete concentration on the task

2. Clarity of goals and reward in mind, and immediate feedback

3. Transformation of time (speeding up / slowing down)

4. Intrinsically rewarding experience

5. Effortlessness and ease

6. Balance between challenge and skills

7. Merged actions and awareness, no self-conscious rumination

8. Feeling of control over the task

How often have I experienced flow? It's hard to say, but I have discovered through trial and error that there are certain things I need to do to make sure I am in the right mental and physical state to create my best work.

The interesting thing about Csikszentmihalyi's eight characteristics of flow is that when you read them in detail, it's obvious that in order to be at your best creatively, you need to take personal responsibility and you need to prepare properly. Let's finish our creative journey by looking at the five steps that will get you closer to creative flow.

THE FIVE STEPS TO FINDING FLOW

1. Find a Place to Create

Where do you create? Think of the people you know who are creative. Musicians go to recording studios, sculptors have studios, and master craftspeople have workshops. The world-famous children's writer Roald Dahl had an almost equally famous shed at the bottom of his garden where he went to write. While there, he always kept the curtains drawn to avoid distractions. He had a brown leather armchair and a wooden tray top that went over his legs. On cold days, he fired up a gas heater and got into a sleeping bag, which also acted as a type of straitjacket to limit his lust to wander. He settled down, pared a few pencils, and smoked a few cigarettes until there was nothing left to do but write. His physical environment enabled him to create.

Where is your creative place? I have my desk in the office of our house. It's in the attic, just under the eaves, and too far for anyone to visit and distract me. When I want to get away from the world, I know I can work there undistracted. I also love working on trains and in coffee shops. I do some of my best creative work sitting in the front of my car, waiting on my two daughters at their various weekly sporting activities. I always sit in the front passenger seat because there is more legroom. When I'm there, I have a feeling of "hiding in plain sight" that makes it easier for me to be creative and productive.

2. Get to Work

To get away from the world, you need to put time aside to create. In a world of endless distractions, this can be difficult. Just think of the amount of time you waste each day on your phone. You need to block out time in your schedule to create, and you need to stick to it.

To start, don't be overly ambitious. Make a small agreement with yourself and stick to it. When I wanted to develop a more creative and productive writing habit, I promised myself I would write every day for thirty minutes for one month. It was amazing how productive it was. I completed over ten thousand words of a book.

Paradoxically, I was more productive because I had less time. Each thirty-minute writing sprint made me more efficient. It also meant I was committed to moving the project along each day and could see the progress.

3. Accept That It Will Take Time

To be really creative, you should practice the ability to pause, and realize that creative work will get better with the addition of time. Creativity is a "game of inches." It can sometimes feel like you are rolling a rock up a hill, inching ever so slowly forward. And that's because you are. Embrace it and celebrate the small successes. Always be willing to take some time to ponder a solution, and don't accept the easy option. I find that if I revisit a draft of writing, after some time I will always be able to improve it. Of course there has to be a cutoff point, but the more you practice, the easier you'll find it to make that decision.

Sometimes when people want to create, they focus on the wrong thing and get daunted and paralyzed by the task that is facing them. My friend Dr. Ciara Losty is a sports psychologist. She has worked with many elite athletes, including a number of Irish Olympians. She has been a great help in enabling me to write. Her advice is simple: "Ask yourself how much time you are going to commit to your work this week, and stick to that commitment." The thought process behind this advice is that great things happen through repeated practice, not by placing focusing on creating something great. If you're worried about creating a masterpiece, it's highly likely you might never get started in the first place.

It's simple. If you put in the time and the hard work, it will get better, but you have to commit to it. I have found that when I adopt this approach, I always do more than what I commit to. And guess what? The work gets better.

Losty's second piece of advice really helps with the creative challenge of rolling the rock up the hill. It is to keep a diary of the work you do. It's what athletes do to get better. It's a way to review your performance with honesty and precision. It helps you see what you're doing well and what you need to improve on.

I keep a spreadsheet. Yes, I'm a real Boy Scout about it. I keep track of when I write, what I write, how much I wrote, how far along I am with my overall goal, and how I felt at the end. In a book like this, five hundred words is 1 percent of fifty thousand: when you keep track, you can see the progress, and that's rewarding. When you hit a target on a day when you're not feeling great, it's like a double reward. I have a second spreadsheet that outlines my overall project progress. It gives details of chapters done, chapters to do, and word counts. It really helps.

You can apply this process to any form of creativity. It doesn't matter if you are preparing a presentation, writing a series of articles, or recording a podcast. Creativity needs a plan and a structure. You need to organize and commit to it.

4. Build Your Confidence by Experimenting

Confidence is the ability to play just to see what will happen next. It is about being open to the possibilities of the work you are creating and following the energy to where it leads you. It means not being too restricted in your outlook and embracing new ideas, sources, and possibilities. It's about not being afraid to experiment. Fearlessness!

When I am giving a storytelling talk at a conference, I will always include a few new slides, a new concept, or a new story. These are the moments I look forward to most when I'm in front of a new audience. And guess what? The stories that work get used over and over again. The stories that work tend to work everywhere for different audiences and in different cultures—that's how powerful and valuable they are.

Equally, the stories that don't work are often shelved after one telling. They are either classified as creative risks or they're reworked until they connect. Either way, it's always worth the risk.

5. Humor

Humor makes everything possible. I started giving communications training courses in the autumn of 2008, and I learned quickly that when people are having a good time, they learn much more.

When people are laughing, they are much more open to suggestions and creativity. It's called "infotainment." I start each course with a simple exercise. I pair people off and I tell them to interview the other person. I give them a number of specific questions they need to find out the answers to, so they can then introduce their partner to the room. The last question is to find out something personal about the other person to share with the group. This always gets a laugh. My favorite one is the time a woman was introducing a man she was paired with. "Oh yeah, the personal thing. This is John, and John used to work in the porn industry." At this point, John went beetroot red and shouted, "I was only laying out the ads!"

Points to Ponder

- You are a creative person. Unless you believe that, you will never embrace it.

- Creativity is not a talent; it is a way of operating. You need to find your creative way of operating to get better results.

- How do you open yourself up to the power of possibility? You need to resource your creativity with different experiences, who you meet, and the information you consume.

- A culture of criticism means a real lack of creativity.

- You need to create a culture where people can take risks and be fearless. If you are a team member, you need to seek out these conditions.

- Questions are the supertool to help you to unlock your creativity. Invest time in framing them correctly. Test and calibrate them carefully and they will help you solve big problems.

Exercises for You

- How many hours can you commit to creative endeavors next week? Set a commitment now and meet it.

- Where is your creative space? Try to find a new one next week and try it out. It doesn't matter where—it could be sitting in the car when your child is at an activity or in your favorite coffee shop.

- How are you resourcing your creativity? Mix up your inspiration for a week. Read a different book. Buy a new magazine. Have a conversation with a new person. Take note of what you learn and how these different sources are feeding your creativity.

- Find three new stories to tell at work next week. It could be a different customer experience, how someone is using your product, or a pain point you were able to solve. Find three fresh stories and start using them.

Understanding the Science behind Stories

Why Does Everyone Love a Good Story?

You now know what a story is and how to fuel your creativity. Finally, in this chapter, we will look at the science behind storytelling to show you why stories work so well.

Our brains are bombarded by stories all day, every day. It doesn't matter if you are catching up with an old friend, reading a great book, listening to a compelling presentation, or binge-watching a series on Netflix.

When you are on the receiving end of a great story, something changes inside of you. Your brain locks into the unfolding narrative—no detail is too small—and you are focused and relaxed in equal measure. You are engaged, and you remember what's going on with great clarity: names, places, moments.

And when you're *telling* a great story, you feel the opposite effect. It feels like you have placed a spell on your audience. You can see the spark in their eyes and you know they are tuned in to you. You have the puppet on a string, and your powers of influence are at their peak.

Let's be clear: you don't need to understand the science of storytelling to tell a story. But you do need to understand it if you really want to comprehend the true power of stories to shape beliefs and behavior, often below conscious awareness.

In the late autumn of 2014, I began to hear murmurings around my office about a podcast everyone was listening to. At first I didn't pay too much notice, but after three days of avoiding the endless analysis and discussion, I had to find out what everyone was obsessing about.

My colleague Lucy informed me the podcast was called *Serial*. It was from the same production team that made *This American Life*, which is now accepted as one of the most influential shows in the history of podcasting.

Serial is about a high school love story that ends in a murder. I was intrigued. "Why is it so good?" I asked.

"It's a great story. I just couldn't stop listening to it," she replied.

The following evening, I had to drive three hours north to Belfast, where I was speaking at a conference. I downloaded a few episodes of *Serial* to my phone to see what all the fuss was about. As I reached the motorway on the outskirts of Dublin, I hit play. From the opening moments, I was completely hooked, so much so that I couldn't get enough.

The podcast tells the story of the murder of an eighteen-year-old Baltimore high school student, Hae Min Lee, in 1999 and the case behind the man convicted of her murder, her former boyfriend, Adnan Syed. There are doubts about his conviction—no one could believe that Syed was a killer, and there are massive holes in the case against him. This is the web of intrigue around which the story unfolds.

My journey north was on a dark and bitterly cold November night, and as I progressed, the driving conditions to Belfast worsened. The one-hundred-mile trip took much longer than I had anticipated, with heavy traffic, wind, and driving rain. As I settled into the podcast, something really odd happened: I didn't mind the terrible driving conditions, the lines of traffic, or the hours I was stuck in the car, because I was glued to the great story that was unfolding on *Serial*.

I was so enthralled that when I eventually parked outside the hotel in Belfast at eleven o'clock, I waited there for another thirty minutes to finish the episode I was listening to. I did the exact same the following evening, at the end of an even longer drive from Belfast to the west of Ireland. From then on, when a new episode arrived each week, I went for a walk to be alone with the story. It was my guilty pleasure.

But why was I so enraptured by the story? What was going on in my brain that was having such a positive and calming effect? And why did I want to hear more? The answer lies in the science behind storytelling, and understanding it will help you to wield this power as a storyteller even more effectively.

When we communicate, our goal is to ensure our audience understands what we are saying, is motivated by it, and acts accordingly. This is too often misunderstood, and just giving people information or the bare facts is not enough to achieve these aims.

There is a moment when you are telling a good story and you realize you are getting through to your audience. You can see they are mentally engaged, focused, and enjoying what you are telling them in equal measure. But what is really happening in this exchange? And why is the story you are telling having such an effect?

In the spring of 2004, Jonathan Cohen and David Tank established the Princeton Neuroscience Institute. Their goal for the institute was for it to act as a spark for new research into and teaching about the nervous system.

In 2010, Professor Uri Hasson and Greg Stephens decided to study the effect of storytelling at the institute. In particular, they wanted to discover scientifically what was really happening in the moments when a storyteller and their audience connected. They chose graduate student Lauren Silbert to help with the research.[11]

As part of their research, Silbert slid her head into an MRI machine and began to tell a story: an epic, unrehearsed story about her junior year in high school. Silbert recreated that year and relived the moments as if they had just happened. Here is the outline of the story.

She met a boy, Amir; she really liked him. But before they started going out, another boy, Charles, asked her to the prom.

On the Saturday of the prom, she went scuba diving with her family. The trip was a disaster. She was supposed to arrive back at 4:00 p.m. and have two hours to get ready, but they had trouble with the engine of their boat. She arrived home at 6:00 p.m., just as Charles was arriving to pick her up.

Because Charles wasn't her boyfriend, it was all very awkward. When she got to the prom, her boyfriend, Amir, was there, but he was drunk. Amir got into a fight with Charles. Almost as soon as she arrived, Lauren left with Amir.

But Amir was in no fit state to be there. When they got outside, he fell in the car park and busted his nose. There was blood everywhere. Lauren had to drive his car while wearing her prom dress. They came upon a car accident, and, in a panic to stop, she gently hit one of the cars. A police officer approached them.

The research team recorded Silbert's story using a special microphone that filtered out the loud hum of the MRI machine. As she spoke, the MRI mapped the pattern of her brain: every movement, every emotion, and every wave captured. Then they played her story back to eleven subjects while their brains were also scanned as they listened, mapping their reactions to Silbert's epic tale.

The results were fascinating. As the story unfolded, the researchers began to see a pattern where the signals being sent out from Silbert's brain as she told the story were being reflected in the brains of the listeners.[12]

This is called neural coupling and describes how the mind of a storyteller is in sync with those listening. It's as if a wire is going out of the storyteller's mind, directly connected with the mind of each listener.

One example of neural coupling was when Lauren spoke about going to the prom. The same areas lit up in her brain as in the brains of her listeners.

This research shows that when you are telling a great story, you are like a master puppeteer controlling the brains of your audience. Neural coupling shows the power of sending a signal and how that signal is a perfect fit for the audience's brain.

Speaker - Listener Neutral Coupling

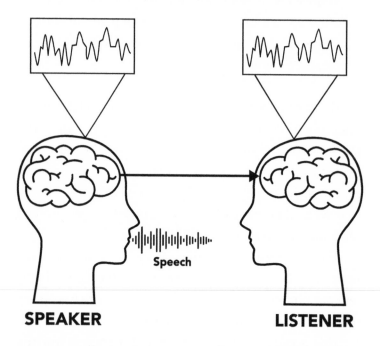

Speech

SPEAKER
LISTENER

Image featured in, "Speaker–listener neural coupling underlies successful communication."[13]

How to Use the Power of Storytelling to Get the Outcome You Want

Storytelling can give you power over the minds of those you are trying to influence.

Imagine you are pitching for an investment in your startup, communicating a major research breakthrough, or looking for additional resources for your team from the board. What do you need to know about the science of storytelling to help you get the results you seek?

The answer lies in the effect stories have on the body. Effective stories trigger hormones that make us feel a certain way. Stories make us feel happy, sad, angry, and excited. They trigger memories and places in our brains we haven't visited in a long time. They help us feel the depths of despair and the heights of joy. It is these feelings that get us to act. They motivate us to change our behavior.

To understand this better, it is best to start by examining the science behind the emotional triggers that stories press. For that, let's look at the endocrine system.[14]

The endocrine system is a collection of glands that produce hormones that regulate, among many things, our metabolism, growth and development, tissue function, sexual function, reproduction, and mood.

The glands are the pituitary, thyroid, parathyroid, adrenal, pancreas, and ovaries (in females) and testicles (in males). Different hormones produce different emotions, and depending on the hormone you trigger, you will get a different reaction from the audience.

There are five main hormones that influence the power of communication. The three most powerful and positive ones we can influence are dopamine, oxytocin, and endorphins. These are described in a TED Talk by David Phillips as "the Angel's Cocktail."[15] This is because triggering any of these hormones allows us to build trust, empathy, understanding, and a bond while increasing the cognition and recall of our audience.

The other two notable hormones are cortisol and adrenaline. When high levels of these are recorded in receivers of information, they are described by Phillips as "the Devil's Cocktail." This is because they make those receiving information irritable, uncreative, intolerant, and prone to bad decisions.

For telling stories, there are three positive hormones: dopamine, oxytocin, and endorphins. There are two negative hormones: cortisol and adrenaline. Let's have a deeper look into each hormone.

Dopamine

Dopamine has many functions in our brain. It helps control movement, what we eat, and how we learn. It is also the "reward hormone." When you drink, smoke, take drugs, or win a bet, that warm rush of pleasure you feel is the release of dopamine.[16]

The suspense of waiting and wondering what's going to happen next in a suspenseful story also triggers dopamine. Think of your favorite series on Netflix and how the moment an episode ends, you instantly click the next episode and bypass the credits, just so you can keep watching the story. That's dopamine.

Television writers and producers know that if they leave us with questions at the end of a season finale, we will be back for the answers in the first episode of the next season.

We do this because of the release of dopamine in our brains. It causes us to feel focused and motivated to find out the ending. A sense of need and want is invoked as we are compelled to know the ending of the story. This can be a powerful tool when telling your story.

Let's see how it works. Let me tell you a story.

A couple of years ago, I was on a business radio show doing an interview about the power of brand storytelling. It was a very engaging interview, and I got to talk in great detail about my passion for storytelling. I got back to my office, and I had a real pep in my step. Just after lunch, one of my colleagues called out that there was a woman on the phone who had heard me on the radio, and she was very keen to talk to me. I pressed the flashing line and introduced myself. She started to speak.

"My name is Lisa, and I'm the communications director at XXX (a big legal firm), in the financial sector here in Dublin. I heard you on the radio talking about storytelling, and you were really great." (I was suitably flattered. Now back to the story.) "We have a problem that needs your approach. It's a really big contract. Can you come in tomorrow to talk about it?" I wanted to crack a joke and say I would come in right now, but we agreed I'd be there the following morning at eleven.

I arrived at the reception of the corporate legal office. It was an impressive glass-and-steel structure with a huge lobby, comfortable sofas, and imposing reception desk. I approached the desk and said I was looking for Lisa, the communications director. I signed in and was asked to take a seat.

A few minutes later, a woman approached. She was tall with frizzy red hair and a gray business suit. It was Lisa. She looked a little addled, was in a rush, and didn't waste any time getting down to brass tacks. "Okay, the meeting. Well, I'm not going to the meeting. It'll be our three directors. They are a serious bunch. Oh, and one of them thinks marketing and PR is a load of rubbish, but if you can convince them, you'll have the gig." She pointed to a room at the end of the lobby. "The meeting is in there. I'll see you after."

I approached the meeting door. It was one of those rooms with a glass panel on either side of the door, so I could see my welcoming party. To say I realized that what I was facing was going to be no fun would be an understatement. Just as I was about to enter the room, I heard a noise over my shoulder. It was Lisa. She was running toward me and raising her voice. In truth, she looked kind of crazy. She said, "There's one more thing that I need to tell you that will help you to get the job. You need to…"

Wouldn't it be really infuriating if I didn't tell you what happened next in this story? I'm not going to tell you. What I have done here is triggered your dopamine. When your dopamine is triggered, you are tuned in. You really want to know what happens next. Every detail matters, and you pick it up with ease.

The next time you are telling a story, try to build suspense, as this will trigger dopamine. Pace your story, making sure to include as many details as possible. Slowly make your way through the story, bringing your audience along with you. This will keep your audience gripped and listening intently to your story.

Oxytocin

Oxytocin is one of the brain's most powerful hormones. It's responsible for social bonding and is often referred to as the "love hormone." Have you ever fallen in love? Oxytocin is that amazing fuzzy feeling you get in the first six weeks of falling in love.

Everything seems amazing, everything your new loved one does is just right, and you feel invincible in their company. Then, after six weeks, the feeling passes. Generating oxytocin through storytelling can help your audience build trust with you. It bonds you and your audience together and helps create a better storytelling experience.

One of the most natural ways to induce oxytocin while telling a story is to reveal something personal about yourself. But this is anathema to how the corporate world operates. If you work in a corporate environment, being personal is viewed as a sign of weakness. You are not supposed to show your personality in how you communicate. You are supposed to stick to the template slides and stay on message.

But eradicating personal stories from how we communicate is counterintuitive to how we are naturally built as people. None of us is a robot. In fact, being personal and personable comes much more naturally to us.

Let me give you an example of a story about myself.

For most of my life, I had a difficult and complicated relationship with my dad, Joe. When I was small, he drank excessively, and it caused me terrible trauma. He gave it up when I was eleven years old, but the scars were deep. I was angry with him, and there was always tension, disagreements, and rows around in our relationship. As a small boy, I learned how to confront trouble head-on, and my dad and his behavior were trouble. As you can imagine, it made for a difficult relationship for both of us and for the rest of our family.

As I approached forty years of age, my dad was turning seventy. By that stage, I was tired of fighting and getting angry, and I decided to do something about it. Through counseling, I learned the power to heal our relationship lay with me. If I could find forgiveness and understanding, the wounds would get better. My previous strategy over the years of waiting for an apology hadn't worked, so I learned how to forgive and understand. It didn't happen overnight. It was definitely a process and took time.

I decided to give him a kiss on the head every time we said goodbye. We were grown men, but I didn't care. I wanted to do it, and it felt good.

When my dad was turning seventy, he and I went for a short break to celebrate. We went to Inishbofin for a couple of days. It's an idyllic small island off the coast of County Galway in the Atlantic Ocean.

When you're forty and you are going away with your seventy-year-old dad, you think long and hard about what rooms you are going to book. Do you book single rooms? Or do you book twin rooms? If you book single rooms, it's as if you're not away together at all. If you book a twin room, it's a little awkward; my dad's snoring could quieten a chainsaw. So I booked a twin room and brought some earplugs. Every night, I'd put them in and fall off to sleep.

Dad and I got on great. He began to open up and talk to me. Our relationship was different; it was softer. The trip was so good that we went on another one the year after, but on that trip he slept a lot, and I was worried about him.

Dad got sick soon after, and the doctors told us he hadn't long to live. During his illness, he opened up to me about his feelings. It seems like an odd thing to say, but we had some amazing, loving conversations when he was in the hospital and in the nursing home.

One day, I walked in and Dad was crying. "What's wrong?" I asked. He looked me straight in the eyes and said, "I'm going to die soon." I paused, and something helped me fight the urge to tell him it would be okay and not to worry.

I asked him how it felt. He thought about that for a moment, and we talked about it. Then I said, "Do you realize what has been happening here for the last few months? All the people who are coming to see you are coming to say thanks for how you helped them in their lives. You have lived a life full of friendship, hard work, and promise. Your life has touched thousands of others, and that's a great thing." He thought about what I said, and he was happy.

A few days later, he slipped into a coma. That was the last meaningful conversation we had. When I got the telephone call one morning in Dublin that he had passed away, I knew he loved me, and I knew that he knew I loved him. Our relationship, which had been so full of hurt, anger, and bad feelings, had softened out into a bond based on love and mutual respect.

I know sharing like this isn't for everyone, but when you reveal something personal about yourself, you build a genuine bond with the audience. Of course, these stories, while being personal, do not have to reveal any of your darkest secrets.

When in front of a corporate audience or in a business setup, why not share a story from your own career journey? If you can be open and generous with your emotions when telling a story, you will engage with your audience and build your relationship with them. It's a very powerful way to communicate.

Endorphins

Be honest. All of us love to laugh. Making someone laugh is one of the greatest storytelling techniques. If you can tell a funny story, people will always have a better chance of remembering it. The ability to introduce humor at the right time and execute it is a sign of a great storyteller.

So what happens when you laugh that makes it easier to process information? Research shows that in group settings, laughter leads to more pleasurable feelings and the release of significantly more endorphins in the brain. This in turn increases the feelings of togetherness, strengthens social bonds, and builds trust.

Think of a time when you laughed almost uncontrollably. What made you do it? You know the feeling: your eyes are watering; you are rocking from side to side; you feel lightheaded. You can remember the feeling vividly. It was an almost out-of-body experience.

Let me tell you a funny story to try to get you to laugh. In November 2015, Robert Dunbar and his colleagues at Oxford University[17] conducted a research study to discover what made funny jokes funnier. Here are three of the funniest jokes that emerged from their research.

SNAIL WITH AN ATTITUDE

A guy is sitting at home when he hears a knock at the door. He opens the door and sees a snail on the porch. He picks up the snail and throws it as far as he can. Three years later, there's a knock on the door. He opens it and sees the same snail. The snail says, "What the hell was that all about?"

TRUE LOVE LASTS FOREVER

It's the World Cup final, and a man makes his way to his seat right next to the pitch. He sits down, noticing the seat next to him is empty. He leans over and asks the man in the next seat if someone will be sitting there. "No," says the neighbor, "the seat is empty." "This is incredible," said the man. "Who in their right mind would have a seat like this for the final and not use it?" The neighbor says, "Well, actually, the seat belongs to me. I was supposed to come with my wife, but she passed away. This is the first World Cup final we haven't been to together since we got married." "Oh, I'm so sorry to hear that. That's terrible...But couldn't you find someone else, a friend, relative, or even a neighbor to take her seat?" The man shakes his head. "No," he says. "They're all at her funeral."

KID VERSUS BARBER

A young boy enters a barbershop, and the barber whispers to his current customer, "This is the dumbest kid in the world. Watch while I prove it to you." The barber puts a dollar bill in one hand and two quarters in the other, then calls the boy over and asks, "Which do you want, son?" The boy takes the quarters and leaves. "What did I tell you?" says the barber. "That kid never learns!" Later, when the customer leaves, he sees the same young boy coming out of the ice cream store. "Hey, son! May I ask you a question? Why did you take the quarters instead of the dollar bill?" The boy licks his cone and replies, "Because the day I take the dollar, the game is over!"

The research shows that when you're funny, the message makes even more of an impact.

I've been giving talks for over ten years, and the good news is that a truly funny story is funny everywhere. It doesn't matter if you are in Beijing or Bratislava, if your story is truly funny, it will work. It's important to experiment with your stories. Like a good comedian, try out new material. The stories that work are golden and will be told over and over again. Remember, it's perfectly okay to reuse a story as long as the audience changes.

Cortisol and Adrenaline

The two hormones associated with stress are cortisol and adrenaline. When you communicate, you should avoid triggering them in your audience at all costs. Often, this happens unknowingly. Let's examine why and how you can avoid falling into this trap.

We are all well acquainted with what stress feels like, but what exactly is the science behind it? Feeling under stress or pressure is part of being alive, and it has many sources. Stress can come from your environment, your body, your own thoughts, and how you look at the world around you.[18]

In communication, there are two main areas where stress can occur. The first is feeling it ourselves as the communicator, and the second is passing it on to others in our audience. It is natural to feel highly stressed around moments of communication such as giving a speech, doing an interview, or presenting to a crucial client.

Research shows that most people fear public speaking more than death.[19] In the words of American actor and comedian Jerry Seinfeld:

> "According to most studies, people's number one fear is public speaking. Number two is death. Death is number two. Does that sound right? This means to the average person, if you go to a funeral, you're better off in the casket than doing the eulogy."

It is perfectly normal to feel nervous and stressed when you are preparing for a presentation. Right now, I want to focus on how to make sure you are not transferring stress onto your audience.

As communicators, I believe we have two simple choices before any piece of communication:

1. Do we choose to communicate with the power of stories that can get right into the solar plexus of the audience and influence them in the most gentle and lasting way?

or

2. Do we share boring, dry facts, using slides with endless lists of bullet points that will be forgotten in seconds and will most likely bore, stress, and confuse our audience?

Doesn't it seem like a simple choice? It seems obvious you would choose stories over facts. But why do we so often lapse into reading out loud what's on the screen or sharing dry information instead of telling a story? One answer is because it's easier, and we are all likely to lapse into something that is easier.

Picture the scene: You've been called into a weekly finance or operations meeting by your manager. You dread it every week. It puts a knot in your stomach. Your manager stands up for twenty minutes and shares spreadsheet after spreadsheet by PowerPoint. You don't understand what he's talking about, and as you struggle to get a grip on the details on the screen by reading them yourself, your manager reads them to you. Have you ever tried to read something when someone is reading it out loud too? I have news—it's almost impossible. Confronted by this situation, you quickly grow stressed, and you are screaming inside your head. Then, just to cope, you shut down, zone out, and play with your phone.

Does that sound familiar? It probably does because either you are on the receiving end of this type of communication or, even worse, you might be the perpetrator of this communications crime.

How do you avoid triggering the stress cycle? As we've learned, all the science shows that stories trump facts and bullet points as a way to communicate. Listen to the science and embrace it.

Start by taking small steps. I understand it is easy to be wedded to a certain way of communicating. If you've always stood in front of a PowerPoint and read the slides, then the thought of not doing so can be daunting. Stressful even.

The first step is to mix up how you are communicating by inserting a few stories. This will take more time and more research, but it will have a more lasting effect on the audience. Make the change and watch what happens. This should give you the confidence to continue your transformation as a storyteller.

Points to Ponder

- To be a great storyteller, it is essential to understand the science behind what happens to people when they hear a story and to use that to your advantage.

- When you tell a story, you have the power to reach into the brains of each and every person in your audience like a puppet master and influence how they think. How will you use that power the next time you get the chance?

- Dopamine is the "Who did it?" hormone. Build suspense and mystery and you will trigger it. It helps with memory, focus, and attention.

- Oxytocin is the trust hormone. Open up and be yourself, and you will trigger it. It will help you build trust, empathy, and understanding with your audience.

- Endorphins are the feel-good hormones. Make people laugh and you will trigger them. They build understanding, empathy, and a sense of togetherness.

- Cortisol and adrenaline are the stress hormones. Understand their corrosive power and avoid triggering them. They make people feel anxious and irritable, and they impair cognition.

Exercises for You

- List the stories you regularly tell about your work. Identify what types of stories they are. Are they suspenseful stories triggering dopamine, empathetic stories triggering oxytocin, or funny stories triggering endorphins?

- Ask yourself if you overly communicate in a way that is dull or even stressful, triggering cortisol and adrenaline. Recognize what you do to create that situation and stop doing it.

- Ask yourself how you could make your stories better. How can you make them even more suspenseful? More empathetic and human? Funnier? Make the changes and watch the reaction the next time you tell them.

The next time you are planning a story, ask yourself: What reaction do you want in the audience? What hormone do you want to trigger? Design your story to get the reaction you want.

2

The Six-Step Magic Slice Process

Getting Started

Now you understand the answers to the three key questions:

1. What is a story and what isn't a story?

2. How do you fuel your storytelling with creativity?

3. How can you be a better storyteller by understanding the science behind how stories work?

We are ready to use my six-step process to enable you to find your Magic Slice. The place where what and how you communicate hits the target every time.

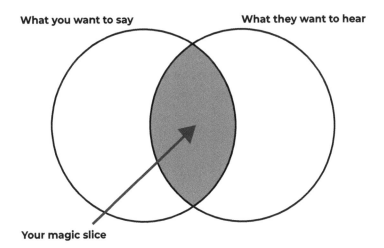

In the new way to communicate, it's not about writing perfect press releases and then waiting for journalists to come to you and offer you an opportunity. It's about creating your own context and finding the tone of voice and creativity that connects with your audience.

It's not about rules. It's about being unique and authentic, having a compelling mission, and finding stories that differentiate you and your cause, product, or service from everyone else. It's about resonating and finding common ground with your audience. It's about empathy, understanding, and continually tuning into those who are listening.

When you decide that you want to create quality stories that matter, there are so many questions:

- How do you craft stories that connect with people and get them to act?

- How do you get people to hear and care about what you are doing?

- How do you tune in to the needs and desires of your audience every day and deliver content that will excite them?

- How do you find your unique tone or style of content that consistently resonates with your potential customers?

In Part 2, we will answer these questions by giving you a new process for discovering and shaping your stories. We will introduce you to the Magic Slice and share with you how to find your unique voice.

Take a look at the graphic below. It outlines the shape of the journey you need to take to discover your Magic Slice.

We will bring you on a step-by-step journey to find your Magic Slice. To get there, you have to do the following:

- Step 1—Find a mission and articulate it.

- Step 2—Tune in to your different audiences.

- Step 3—Create your Magic Slice Topics for stories.

- Step 4—Create your Magic Slice Statement.

- Step 5—Generate compelling stories.

- Step 6—Revise and edit your stories in the light of experience and the changing environment.

Let's get started.

Step 1
Find a Mission and
Articulate It

Your Magic Slice needs to be driven by the mission of your organization. Your mission is why you exist and what you are trying to achieve. To be a great storyteller and to communicate from your Magic Slice with ease, you need to be driven by a mission. Let's discover how.

Communicating through stories is a powerful way to achieve your goals. But the first step to ensuring that you and your team have a "story instinct" is to ground your communications into the beating heart of your organization.

In practice, this means having a mission statement that is clear, unambiguous, and easy to communicate. It should be specific to your organization or brand and be easily recognizable as *your* mission statement, not that of your competitor or a company in a different industry. It should be short, to the point, and written in plain English with no jargon or buzzwords.

Right now, do you have a written mission or vision statement? What does it look like? It's okay if you don't. It might be easier to create a new mission statement than to reimagine one that isn't working.

Knowing your mission, your purpose, and the reason you exist is central to communicating clearly. It is essential that your mission be grounded in reality and be authentic and achievable. Sometimes brands engage in mission statement optics by adopting a lofty purpose merely for public relations and corporate social responsibility purposes. This rarely works, and your customers and other audiences can see through it.

If you adopt a mission that fits your organization, and which you have the drive, motivation, and ability to achieve, it will be a powerful driving force.

But even when you are motivated to change how you communicate and become clearer, it's still easy to get confused. People often get hung up on the difference between mission and vision statements. We're not going to do that. We're going to focus on helping you to have a mission at the heart of your brand or organization, and we're going to capture it in a statement.

What is a mission? It's a compelling reason or purpose that drives what you do. In the words of Simon Sinek, it's what you do and why you do.

Let's start perfecting your mission.

Your Mission as a Creed

Every organized religion in the world has a service, a Mass, prayers, or some type of organized worship. I was raised Catholic and central to Catholic teaching is the Mass.

As a boy, I got bored at Sunday Mass, and I used to keep myself occupied by observing the rituals we were asked to participate in. One particular part of the Mass intrigued me: the recital of a prayer called the Apostles' Creed. Before reciting the prayer, everybody stood up and made the sign of the cross on their forehead, their lips, and their heart.

The creed begins with "I believe in" and then goes through a description of everything Catholics believe. When people recite the prayer, they are saying clearly what their purpose is and why they are there.

I remember that when I figured out what it was all about, I used to whisper every time, "This is why we're all here," before my mother told me to be quiet.

To have a unified purpose written down in a way that is understandable for a group or tribe is quite powerful. It's why certain songs become unofficial anthems of a cause, a team, a country, or a movement. They have the ability to bring people together, and in the shorthand of a few verses. The ballad "Waltzing Matilda" was written by the Australian poet Banjo Paterson in August 1895 and became the anthem of the settlers. It conveyed what it meant to live a frontier life.

In Japanese business culture, they have a tradition of the daily *Chorei*, pronounced "cho-ray." At a *Chorei*, team members gather for a morning stand-up meeting, often citing the company mission before outlining their key tasks for that day. The purpose of a *Chorei* is to create a deeper team bond around a shared mission or purpose and what everyone's role means in achieving that. It introduces great clarity.

How to Perfect Your Mission

What are the characteristics of a great mission statement? It should:

- Be no longer than a paragraph

- Be specific to your business or your work

- Be ambitious, looking to the future and promoting great standards

- Have a unique twist that only your organization can bring

And remember—no jargon. A perfect stranger should understand what you're trying to achieve. Industry language, acronyms, and buzzwords only serve to keep people out. Let's look at some good and bad examples.

IKEA

IKEA is the largest furniture manufacturer and retailer in the world. This is its mission statement:

> "At IKEA, our vision is to create a better everyday life for the many people. Our business idea supports this vision by offering a wide range of well-designed, functional home furnishing products at prices so

low that as many people as possible will be able to afford them."[20]

Notice how it mentions "the many people." It is clearly saying *it* wants to serve as many people as possible with great design at low prices.

IKEA delivers on that promise by developing insights into the lives of its customers. In a process that can sometimes seem like alchemy, it turns those customer insights into cleverly designed and affordable furniture and household items that are sold and shipped in ready-to-assemble flat packs. It has completely revolutionized how home furnishing is done and created a cultural phenomenon that stretches far beyond its brand.

IKEA's purpose is rooted in its foundation story. Its founder, Ingvar Kamprad, was born in the 1920s on a small farm in isolated rural Sweden. Kamprad first got into the home-furnishings business to help people with little or no money whose only chance to acquire furniture was either to make it themselves or inherit it.

The company name is directly linked to this. The letters in IKEA represent I and K for Ingvar Kamprad (the founder's name), E for Elmtaryd (the farm where he grew up), and A for Agunnaryd (his hometown). His community in the Småland province believed in hard work, frugality, and living as equals—all linked to a feeling of shared poverty. These values would become part of IKEA's ethos.

Kamprad stayed committed to IKEA's mission even when, in 1955, some competitors, disgruntled by IKEA's lower prices, organized suppliers to boycott the company.

Rather than break his promise and begin charging customers more, he decided to change how the company tackled the problem. He brought design in-house and turned to new manufacturers in Eastern Europe.

Lego

Lego is an iconic brand and the largest toy manufacturer in the world. It doesn't just sell toys. Included in its mission is a desire to encourage:

> "The development of children's creativity through play and learning."[21]

To deliver on that promise, it designs sets of interconnecting blocks that can be assembled in a myriad of ways.

But in 2004, Lego was in danger of going out of business. Why? Because, in the words of CEO Jørgen Vig Knudstorp, Lego had lost touch with its mission. "It had lost its way, in terms of understanding its own self-identity. What is Lego uniquely about?" To discover the answer to that question, he made the brand go back to basics, starting with that fundamental question, "Why do you exist?" and moving to "only doing the things where we had a unique advantage."[22]

To get back to its leading position in the toy industry, Knudstorp put a strategy in place to turn the company around, which included divesting or discontinuing products that were not in line with its core mission. For example, it sold its video game development arm and four theme parks. When it lost its way, its mission acted as a touchstone, a guiding light. It had gotten off track, but when it got back to what its mission was, it began to thrive again. There is a huge lesson in that.

Warby Parker

Warby Parker is another great example of a newer brand powered by a compelling mission statement. Let's take a deeper look.

It was co-founded by Neil Blumenthal and three class-mates in a Wharton MBA program. They started talking about the high price of designer eyewear, and they realized there was an opportunity. The brand name was derived from the names of two characters in a journal kept by novelist Jack Kerouac—Warby Pepper and Zagg Parker. This is its mission:

> Warby Parker was founded with a rebellious spirit and a lofty objective: to offer designer eyewear at a revolutionary price, while leading the way for socially conscious businesses.
>
> Every idea starts with a problem. Ours was simple: glasses are too expensive. We were students when one of us lost his glasses on a backpacking trip. The cost of replacing them was so high that he spent the first semester of grad school without them, squinting and complaining. (We don't recommend

this.) The rest of us had similar experiences, and we were amazed at how hard it was to find a pair of great frames that didn't leave our wallets bare. Where were the options?

It turns out there was a simple explanation. The eyewear industry is dominated by a single company that has been able to keep prices artificially high while reaping huge profits from consumers who have no other options.

We started Warby Parker to create an alternative.

By circumventing traditional channels, designing glasses in-house, and engaging with customers directly, we're able to provide higher-quality, better-looking prescription eyewear at a fraction of the going price.

We believe that buying glasses should be easy and fun. It should leave you happy and good-looking, with money in your pocket.

We also believe that everyone has the right to see.

Almost one billion people worldwide lack access to glasses, which means that 15% of the world's population cannot effectively learn or work. To help address this problem, Warby Parker partners with nonprofits like VisionSpring to ensure that for every pair of glasses sold, a pair is distributed to someone in need.

There's nothing complicated about it. Good eyewear, good outcome.[23]

It is a wonderful mission statement. While it is longer than a paragraph, its actual mission is captured in the first sentence:

"To offer designer eyewear at a revolutionary price, while leading the way for socially conscious businesses."

The rest of this brief, 278-word statement gives great insight and clarity into what the company is about. It passes all the tests. It's short, is in plain English, is specific to its business, and shows real differentiation. It also gives context to how it started and how it achieves its mission:

"By circumventing traditional channels, designing glasses in-house, and engaging with customers directly, we're able to provide higher-quality, better-looking prescription eyewear at a fraction of the going price."

There it is in black and white. Mission always looks so easy when it's done well.

But there are many more bad examples than good ones.

Bad Mission Statements

Huge companies are not immune from producing terrible mission statements. Sometimes, the bigger you are, the harder it can be to define a clear purpose that can unite people. Bad examples include Sony, whose mission statement reads:

"To be a company that inspires and fulfills your curiosity. Our unlimited passion for technology, content, services, and relentless pursuit of innovation drives us to deliver ground-breaking new excitement and entertainment in ways that only Sony can."[24]

It's not very specific. Its opening line is so weak, it's comical. Don't we all want to inspire and fulfill your curiosity? If you didn't know what Sony did, you wouldn't be entirely sure based on this.

McDonald's mission statement includes this line:

"Our worldwide operations are aligned around a global strategy called the Plan to Win, which centers on an exceptional customer experience—People, Products, Place, Price and Promotion."[25]

You can spot a mile off why that's bad. It's dry, technical, not industry-specific, and could be something from a bland corporate instruction manual.

Patagonia—Example of Excellence

Before you work on your own mission, I want to take a deeper look at an organization driven by a great mission. Patagonia is one of the most dynamic mission-driven companies of the last fifty years.

For over five decades, Patagonia founder Yvon Chouinard has been one of the most dynamic and compassionate entrepreneurs in the world. His business is proof of the power of a compelling mission and of telling stories about making that mission a reality.

Since its inception, Patagonia has spent decades perfecting the products it sells. It has researched different materials, colors, working environments, and environmental ethics to create products it is proud of and ones that will promote a safer environment.

Patagonia's mission is to:

> "Build the best product, cause no unnecessary harm, use business to inspire and implement solutions to the environmental crisis."[26]

Patagonia founder Yvon Chouinard was born in Maine, in 1938, into a large French-Canadian community that had moved south of the border to find work. His father, from Quebec, had just three years at school before he had to leave to work on the family farm at the age of nine.

The Chouinards moved to California in 1946. Yvon's mother hoped the dry climate would ease her husband's asthma, but it wasn't a comfortable transition for young Yvon, who spent much of his time skipping classes.

Settling down after the move wasn't helped by the fact that Yvon was hopeless at whatever sport he tried. He was too short for basketball, not strong enough for football, and didn't have the coordination for baseball.

In 1953, as a fourteen-year-old, he began rock climbing. The sport wasn't popular in America at the time, and he soon realized that simply by climbing he would be the best in his class, because nobody else was doing it.

He also loved nature and the outdoors. He joined a local falconry club. His love for climbing and the environment grew in tandem. The excitement and intensity of rappelling down sheer cliffs had him instantly hooked.

When he was old enough, Chouinard and his friends let their adventurous spirits roam free by going on trips of their own to live in the outdoors, climb, and rappel down rocks. They hopped freight trains to travel from the west end of the San Fernando Valley to the nearby sandstone cliffs of Stoney Point in California.

Yvon graduated from high school in 1956. He had big ambitions for his climbing obsession, and a year later, he bought a secondhand anvil, a hammer, tongs, and a coal-fired forge. He wanted to make his own equipment to tackle the Yosemite mountains' big walls on multiday ascents.

Previously, American climbers had used cheap European pitons (a spike with a loop for rope at one end) to wedge into cracks. The problem was that European pitons were made from a soft steel and couldn't withstand longer, harder ascents. Chouinard's harder steel pitons could be used over and over again. He could make two in an hour, and he sold them at $1.50 each. Later in the year, when he was eighteen, he borrowed $850 to buy a drop-forging die to make hardened carabiners. Chouinard Inc. was in business.

Over the next few years, he lived for the seasons. In the winter, he hammered out climbing equipment in his workshop, and in the summer he climbed. Money was always tight, so much so that he would often retrieve bottles from bins to redeem the deposits. One summer, he claims, he survived on a couple of cases of cat food. He spent two-thirds of the year in a sleeping bag, sheltering under boulders.

In 1964, he made the first ascent of El Capitan, the Yosemite climbing landmark, the hardest big wall climb in the world at the time. He also printed his first catalog, warning customers not to expect a speedy delivery from May to November. His free spirit and his ethos were beginning to show in his business. This would be a trend.

He hired friends to help design and build the climbing gear, but he still thought of the business as a way to pay the bills for his climbing trips. By 1970, the quality of his work meant Chouinard Equipment had become the largest supplier of climbing hardware in the US. But it had, in Chouinard's own words, started down the path to becoming an environmental villain.

The increasing popularity of climbing meant that more and more hard steel pitons were being hammered into the cracks, and it was destroying the very walls that climbers loved. Even though pitons accounted for 70 percent of Chouinard's business, he resolved to phase them out.

He made his first environmental move. In 1972, he published an essay in the catalog advocating a more environmental approach by using the British climbers' delicate aluminum chocks instead of steel pitons.

It wasn't just America's West Coast where Yvon enjoyed climbing: he traveled the world. In 1970, during a winter trip in Scotland, he bought a rugby shirt to wear while climbing. This was a far cry from his traditional uniform made up of cut-off chinos and white dress shirts, usually bought from a thrift store.

This impulse purchase would change his life. This new top, built to withstand the brute force of a rugby match, withstood the climb. The collar prevented hardware slings from cutting into Chouinard's neck. He knew he was onto something. Back home, he continued to wear rugby jerseys while climbing. It caught on, and before he knew it, he had started a new fashion trend and a brightly decorated rugby jersey with a good collar was in high demand.

To keep up with growing demand, Chouinard ordered jerseys from Umbro in England. They sold out. He then began ordering from New Zealand and Argentina. They sold out too. He saw clothing as a way to support his equipment business. By 1972, the business had expanded further. It was now selling raincoats and bivouac sacks from Scotland and boiled-wool gloves and mittens from Austria.

As the clothing side to the company grew, he decided it needed a unique name. In 1973, the Patagonia brand was born. A name that brings to mind "romantic visions of glaciers tumbling into fjords, jagged windswept peaks, gauchos, and condors."

Today, Patagonia is one of the world's leading environmentally friendly clothing brands, but it wasn't always that way. In 1991, it faced a crisis. Up to that point, it had been growing rapidly and was, in fact, one of the fastest-growing private companies in the US. Then a recession hit and the bank called in the revolving loan. To pay off the debt, Patagonia had to lay off 20 percent of its workforce, many of them close friends. It had become dependent on growth it couldn't sustain.

Chouinard took his senior managers on a retreat to Patagonia, and they returned with a new focus and a commitment to their environmental mission. Today the company reaches far beyond clothing and is committed to teaching and training the next generation of environmental activists. Patagonia is doing this to continue its mission of finding a solution to the environmental crisis.

In 2005, Chouinard published a philosophical manual for employees to lean on as the company grew. That manual became the bestselling book *Let My People Go Surfing: The Education of a Reluctant Businessman*. It captures Yvon Chouinard's unique story and goes deep into his mission and philosophy of business. It is a manual for a whole new generation of activists and ethical entrepreneurs.

Lessons from Patagonia

What storytelling lessons can we learn from Patagonia's focus on its mission and how it tells its story? Here are a few to ponder:

1. Live Your Culture Every Day

Patagonia's mission statement is simple. One short sentence comprehensively tells us who it is, what it is about, and what it wants to achieve.

"Build the best product, cause no unnecessary harm, use business to inspire and implement solutions to the environmental crisis."

It doesn't stop there. As you explore its website, its blog, and its social media, you begin to see that Patagonia embodies its mission statement in everything it does. Its background and how it runs its company demonstrates this. A lot of its content and projects have its mission statement at its heart. Patagonia is passionate about what it believes in, and it is clear to see. Its mission statement is not put together to make its company look good. Instead, it is a statement of intent. It is designed to act as a constant reminder of the good it is doing and continually trying to do.

2. Build a Network of Brand Ambassadors and Use Them

Patagonia has a group of over ninety dedicated brand ambassadors. These ambassadors aren't famous climbers or snowboarders. They are users of Patagonia clothing in various outdoor activities and are enthusiasts in their chosen fields. They produce content for the brand's blog and social media accounts based on their activities and what they are currently up to. This content is broken up into each ambassador's respective area. Patagonia has focused on its target audiences and uses its brand ambassadors as a means of engagement.

3. Engage with Your Audience

With many companies, once you have bought the product, your interaction with them is over. This is not the case with Patagonia. It constantly engages with the audience. This is achieved through clothing recycling initiatives, an email newsletter, feedback forms, or public outreach initiatives.

This demonstrates that Patagonia is enthusiastic about engaging with all those who visit the site and constantly wants feedback on how to improve. It also shows it is passionate about what it believes in and is keen to spread the word. It shows it is a brand that keeps people at the heart of what it does. This makes customers feel included in the process and therefore makes them more engaged with the brand.

Here are some of the storytelling tools that Patagonia uses to communicate:

Clothing Initiatives

Patagonia's interaction with customers does not end once its clothes have been purchased. Patagonia has introduced the Worn Wear initiative. It allows Patagonia users to buy used clothing, repair their own damaged clothing, or trade in clothing and receive credit to put toward a new or used garment. It is another embodiment of Patagonia's mission statement. It demonstrates its commitment to its cause.

Stories that Travel the Country— the Patagonia Truck

As part of the Worn Wear campaign, Patagonia constructed a purpose-built truck to travel around America to repair clothes on the move. The converted biodiesel vehicle was kitted out with industrial sewing machines, with two of Patagonia's seamstresses on board for the journey. This truck, built with environmentally friendly and reusable material, is a unique embodiment of what Patagonia stands for. The truck also acts as a storyteller, capable of being the focal point of many stories as it travels cross-country.

Immersing Your Audience in Your Culture

One of the many things Patagonia does well is video content. Whether long or short, Patagonia routinely uploads visually impressive and thought-provoking videos on a range of topics. These videos allow audiences to see Patagonia products up close and to join brand ambassadors on their adventures around the world, and provide a sneak peek into the lives of those who are behind the clothes.

Impart Your Wisdom to Those Who Want to Listen

Patagonia reaches out to those who believe in its cause. Since 1994, every two years, Patagonia has held what it calls a tools conference. It gathers thought leaders and experts from both nonprofit and for-profit organizations. They share their expertise with advocates from grassroots environmental groups that Patagonia has connected with through its grants program. These conferences have trained an entire generation of activists.

In 2016, Patagonia published *Tools for Grassroots Activists: Best Practices for Success in the Environmental Movement.* This includes advice and knowledge from everything Patagonia has learned over the years, specifically at its tools conferences, packaged into a neat book about how to succeed in building grassroots environmental campaigns.

Patagonia also connects with those who are not customers. It has a dedicated page on its website where people can request a representative from Patagonia to speak at an event. This is part of Patagonia's mission and shows how passionate it is about what it believes in. It wants to get its message out and share its ideas and experiences with the broader community.

With these initiatives, Patagonia wants to inspire its audience and enable them to create ideas as to how they can be more effective in solving the environmental crisis.

Points to Ponder

- Your mission should drive everything you do. It is the reason your brand or organization exists. The more cluttered it is, the more confused your project will be. The clearer it is, the easier everything will be.

- A great mission will drive all of the important metrics in your business, not just storytelling. Everything should be easier with a great mission: hiring, finance, revenue generation, and new product development.

- For your mission to work, it must have these characteristics:

    o Be no longer than a paragraph

    o Be specific to your business or your work

    o Be ambitious, looking to the future and promoting great standards

    o Have a unique twist that only your organization can bring

- Do your people regularly talk about the mission of your organization when they address one of your audiences? They should.

Exercise for You

Here is an exercise you can do by yourself or with colleagues. To have a great Magic Slice, you need to have a short, relevant, punchy, and compelling mission statement. Remember the guidelines listed above.

To do this exercise, you will need some sticky notes and markers—mobile thoughts are always best.

1. Write down all the reasons you think your organization exists. One reason per sticky note. Place them all on a wall so they can be viewed together.

2. Examine the list and separate it into the things that are specific to your industry and the things that anyone can say about their business.

3. Now look at the list that is specific to your industry and expand on it. How can you make the things on this list specific to your organization or brand? This will be a list of things you are recognized as doing well.

4. Take the new list of things specific to your industry that you do well and make them more ambitious. Ask yourself how you could rewrite it to be positive, motivating, and ambitious. You should have plenty of raw material for a great mission statement now.

Step 2
Tune In to Your Different Audiences

To define your Magic Slice, you need to know everything possible about the different target audiences you need to reach with your stories. You can only communicate clearly to them when you know exactly who they are: their needs, desires, likes, and dislikes. Let's discover the best ways to achieve that.

To meet the needs of your target audiences, you need to understand clearly who they are, what they do, and how they are motivated. Think of yourself as a detective. Your job is to find out every piece of available evidence on how your different audiences behave.

Let's start by defining exactly what an audience is.

An audience is a group of people who watch, listen, read, or consume the same thing.

When you are communicating, you will have multiple and different audiences to connect with. These are usually divided by whether they are internal and within your company or external and outside of your direct control. Examples of internal audiences can include employees, investors, and company directors. External audiences include the media, key suppliers, and your customers.

Here are the four questions you need to ask about any audience you want to communicate with:

1. How would you describe your audience in a sentence?

2. What are the defining traits of the people in your audience? What traits, habits, or characteristics put them in your audience? It could be their age; location; taste; interest or desire in a fashion, hobby, or activity; income; occupation; or gender.

3. Who or what influences them?

4. What are their pain points, and how do you cure them?

There is no point if you are the only one who knows this information—everyone on your team should know it too. For your story to truly resonate with an audience, they need to be able to empathize with you, to see *themselves* in the way you communicate with them. Let me tell you a story about how I first learned the importance of knowing the audience.

"If we are going to manufacture shoes that women love, we have to understand everything about how they think."

Michael Walsh, Dubarry Shoes

Lessons from Dubarry Shoes

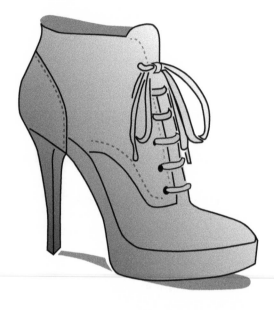

In 1996, I started my first job in marketing out of college. It was as the junior marketing assistant in Dubarry Shoes, a well-known brand based in my hometown of Ballinasloe in the west of Ireland.

A few days after starting, I was in the office of my boss, Michael Walsh. Michael was about ten years older than me and intensely interested in shoes. I noticed, on the ground just inside the office door, a large stack of glossy women's magazines. I joked with him about his choice of reading material. He pretty soon wiped the smirk off my face. "It's essential reading. If we are going to manufacture shoes that women love, we have to understand everything about how they think. Get reading."

It was a formative lesson in getting to know an audience. Like a detective, I started keeping a file of the audience discoveries I made: advertisements from competing brands, interesting images and features, and notes of useful insights into how the audience operated. Back then, we had multiple audiences and a tiny budget.

In Ireland, the "back to school" season is massive for shoe companies. And back then, you could make or break a whole trading year by how you performed in August. One of my jobs as marketing assistant was to get a deeper understanding of our school-going customers and to communicate this to the senior manager. The way they looked at it, I was the perfect person for the job because I wasn't long out of school myself.

To aid my investigation, I conducted focus groups in schools. I always brought a large box of the latest styles with me, which I would lay out on a table and cover with a cloth. The sessions started with a very broad discussion about fashion, shopping trends, and preferences. I eventually got each student to give a specific appraisal of the individual shoes on the table. Each style was discussed and scored. The insights we gleaned in these sessions were invaluable, and the participants got a voucher for a free pair of shoes for their trouble. I learned about the decision processes of our customers by doing this more than anything else.

One day, in the depths of summer, Michael called me into his office. It was July, and the crucial back-to-school campaign was just around the corner. He was worried that we didn't have a winning shoe in the range targeted at teenage girls. The previous day, the company's chief designer had secured an order for a radical new sole at a trade show in Milan. He showed it to me. It had what was called an extended rand around the bottom, like the tube on a bicycle tire protruding around the sole of the shoe. We needed to test it with a focus group, but all the schools were on summer holidays.

We came up with a plan. Every summer in Ireland, children go to parts of the country for special camps where they speak only our native language. It's called the Gaeltacht (pronounced "gale-tocked"). I was dispatched to a Gaeltacht in Connemara, a remote and beautiful spot an hour west of the city of Galway, with the "golden shoe" to discover if it was going to be a winner.

My only problem was that the whole process had to be conducted in the Irish language. I muddled through with my pidgin Irish, asking as probing questions as I could, before I headed home. When I arrived back, I was called to Michael's office. To my surprise, there waiting for me were the CEO, the CFO, the head of materials, the marketing manager, and the head of design, all wanting to know how I got on. I gave them my assessment. I thought the shoe would do fine, but it wasn't going to be a blockbuster success.

My trip to the Gaeltacht taught me a huge lesson. I was struck by how my standing in the company had skyrocketed, albeit temporarily, that afternoon. The full senior management team was waiting on me and hanging on my every word. Why? All because I had fresh consumer insights and knew things about the audience that they didn't. The power of having this information never left me.

Let's figure out the ways you can discover all you need to know about your audiences.

Start at the End—Judge Your Success by How the Audience Feels

When you understand your audience at a deep level, you will know if your story is connecting with them. One really good way of knowing you are communicating from your Magic Slice is to start at the end and imagine the reaction your story might get from an audience.

Let's take it one step further. Imagine if I told you that you had to face your audience in person, perform your story live, and impress them. How scared would you be to step out from the cloak of the internet and actually face your audience? There is nothing like an experience to really enforce learning. It works because there is nowhere to hide.

One of the reasons I love telling stories in public is because when you are face-to-face with the audience, you will always know whether or not your story is working. You will see it in their faces and you will feel the reaction.

There are three distinct audience reactions to stories that are communicated from your Magic Slice. When you get them, you know you are communicating from there. They are:

1. "This is a new voice."

2. "You're saying what I've been thinking."

3. "I've never thought of this before."

Let's explore these in a little more detail.

Reaction 1—"This Is a New Voice"

If you get the reaction "This is a new voice," you know you have found a way to communicate that is fresh and engaging and stands out from the crowd. It is not that you are saying things people haven't said before—this is about *how* you communicate. You are taking a new approach. How you communicate is fresh, original, and stands out.

PADDY POWER

When Ken Robertson first joined the marketing department of Paddy Power in 1999, it was a high-street bookmaker like many of its competitors. The company was started in 1988 when three smaller Dublin bookmakers merged. Robertson was given the job of heading up brand communications. Paddy Power needed to do something different to stand out from a crowded field. Robertson quickly became the company's first self-styled "Head of Mischief."

Mischief became the byword for Paddy Power's brand personality. It specialized in publicity stunts that captured the public's attention and got them talking about Paddy Power. As a brand, it pioneered the "This is a new voice" approach.

During the 2012 European Football Championship finals in Poland and Ukraine, Denmark was playing Portugal and had made a spirited comeback from two goals down to being just one behind. With ten minutes to go, Denmark attacked down the right. A deep cross was met at the far post by the forehead of Danish striker Nicklas Bendtner. It flashed into the net off the left upright. As Bendtner ran away to the adulation of the Danish fans, he raised his shirt with his left hand to reveal the waistband of his underwear. The Paddy Power logo was crystal clear for millions of TV viewers.

Bendtner was fined €100,000 ($118,000) by the Union of European Football Associations (UEFA) as the stunt was in contravention of the strict rules on sponsorship imposed by European football's governing body. It was a small price to pay for the media coverage that Paddy Power received for the stunt. Ironically, Bendtner had forgotten to reveal his underwear when he scored Denmark's first goal in the game, and they went on to lose in the eighty-seventh minute. But Paddy Power didn't care because it got its voice on the story. Ken Robertson added the following very cheesy comment to Paddy Power's official press statement after the game: "I'm truly delighted for Nicklas, what a stunning performance tonight. I've no doubt that the luck of the Irish, thanks to our lucky underpants, helped him find the back of the net twice!"[27]

Other examples of Paddy Power's stunts include an image it released on the eve of the 2014 World Cup of felled trees in the Amazon rainforest, which spelled out the message "Come on England PP." It was a hoax, but it was so convincing that thousands were duped. The firm claimed it was highlighting the plight of the environment. It was also a convenient way to get free media coverage.

Paddy Power has always been willing to take risks in pursuit of its unique brand voice, and many of these stunts have been in poor taste. This can be a tricky and dangerous way to communicate when the audience perceives that you want to get coverage at all costs.

In 2015, Paddy Power ran an advertisement during the Oscar Pistorius murder trial in which it offered "Money back if he walks" for punters betting on the outcome. The advert showed Pistorius mocked up as an Oscar statuette, with the headline "It's Oscar Time." The UK's advertising watchdog, the ASA, received a record 5,525 complaints about the campaign.[28] Paddy Power took the unusual step of ordering the campaign to be pulled immediately, saying it was likely to cause widespread offense.

Also in 2015, it sent an empty container through Calais, at the height of the migrant crisis, with the slogan "Immigrants jump in the back, but only if you're good at sport."[29] I would argue this way to communicate is not for the fainthearted and is designed to cause offense and get noticed. There are easier ways to have a new voice.

IRISH NATIONAL POLICE FORCE

One good example of the positive "This is a new voice" approach is the Irish national police force, which is known as An Garda Síochána. On its social media accounts, the organization is not afraid to share humor and human interest stories along with serious crime stories. It shares images of stupid crimes and ridicules those responsible without naming them, such as the person who tied a huge bed onto the roof of their car and then drove on a motorway. It reunites people with lost wedding rings and shows images of lost dogs handed in to police stations. But it also shows recovered drugs and weapons from crime gangs. It's a balancing act, but it works because it has personality and it's brave.

Like most national police forces, the Irish police force wasn't known for its warm and engaging personality. Police work is serious. Deciding to be a new voice is a risk, and being a police force that communicates on social media with wit, personality, and empathy is difficult. It is a genuine new voice.

Ask yourself how you could become a new voice in your sector. What could you do? What would stand out from the crowd? And could you do it consistently?

Reaction 2—"You're Saying What I've Been Thinking"

This reaction is what is known as an "aha" moment. It is when you tap into something that everybody has been thinking. When you get this reaction, the difference is that you didn't just have a hunch—you acted on it. And you shared it in a way that resonated with your audience based on an innate understanding of how they think.

Great storytellers do this instinctively. They follow their hunch about a mood, a detail, or an opinion. They share it, and the audience loves it. It's almost as if it's an inner moment of clarity, shining new light on a subject.

Hunches are a powerful tool in communications and cast real light on how the brain works. They go deep into our subconscious and so are worthy of some examination.

Imagine the scene: You are away from the office on a sunny afternoon, relaxing in your favorite coffee shop, a million miles from your daily grind. You are reading a magazine and flicking through your social media accounts on your phone. A thought occurs about work. Maybe something you've read flashes an idea in your head, or something pops up online that grabs your attention. At first the thought just bubbles up in your brain, but gradually it takes hold and becomes a full-scale intellectual ambush.

The idea that started as a gentle nag gradually gets more intense. By the time you can't ignore it anymore, you are having a conversation with yourself, often using language like:

Somebody should do that...somebody should really say something about that...or somebody really needs to act on that.

What has happened? You've had a hunch. In that moment, you've directly tapped into your experience and knowledge about your work and made a snap decision.

What is a hunch? It's a feeling based on intuition rather than a fact. It's a powerful force. People with well-tuned instincts, who know their topic really well, have hunches all the time. In the words of legendary Hollywood screen director Frank Capra, "A hunch is your creativity trying to tell you something." It doesn't matter if you continue to suppress your creative urges; they will find a way out, and hunches are one of those ways.[30]

How did your hunch happen? Your brain is a complex computer, and when a hunch occurs, it's as if that file you are searching for among the millions available is returned to you in a nanosecond. It gives you what looks and, more importantly, what feels like the right answer in an instant.[31]

We all know how difficult it is to make clear decisions. Every day is filled with endless choices and a myriad of digital and other distractions. Clear decision-making can often seem impossible. We try to find the right information, the best advice, and then we have to make a choice. When you have a hunch, it's like a reflex action that taps directly into what you believe, and you can make complex decisions really quickly.

So what happens in most cases when you get a hunch about your work? In a magic moment, you have wired into that special place where the world intersects with your deeply held opinions and knowledge. You have a powerful feeling, an urge to act, an answer to an impossible problem. What do you do? The possibilities are endless, but more often than not, you do nothing. You flick the page, sip your coffee, and let the moment pass. Maybe it'll be lost forever.

Hunches are seldom timed correctly. They will come over us at the most inconvenient, and sometimes inappropriate, times. They often happen when we relax our brains and discover a different thought pattern, or maybe when we are stressed out at the end of a busy week and have reached our elastic limit.

The stories and content we share that are based on our hunches are extremely powerful, and we should act on them. Emotions are a crucial part of successful communications, and storytelling and hunches give us gift-wrapped emotional content that taps into our creativity.

My advice is simple:

Don't expect someone else to act on your hunch.

If you have an instinct for your cause, you've been sent a powerful message from your intuition. That means you have a jump start on everybody else. Act on it and you will often get amazing results.

IFA SCANDAL

In the autumn of 2015, a big scandal broke in Ireland. It emerged that the Irish Farmers' Association (IFA)—the largest representative organization for farmers in the country—was paying exorbitant salaries to its leadership. Senior staff resigned, and the story raged in the media.

On the Wednesday of the second week of the scandal, my wife, a journalist, was on a late-night radio show discussing the crisis at the IFA. I was at home, slumped in front of the television after a long day. I had delivered a tricky communications strategy session for a client and had a late meeting with another who had a launch the next day.

I can remember being extremely tired when, soon after ten o'clock, the hunch struck me. It went something like this: *They are handling the public relations of this mess very poorly. Somebody should really point out what can be learned from it.*

I ignored my hunch for a second, but it came back even more pronounced, this time with a little voice on my shoulder saying, *This "somebody" is you. This is your hunch. Don't expect anybody else to act on your hunch.*

So, almost in spite of myself, I opened my laptop and tapped out a blog post entitled "The 5 Public Relations Lessons We Can Learn from the IFA Salary Scandal." I published it and shared it online.

Then something interesting happened. The next morning, my phone rang. It was a national TV reporter called Fran McNulty, who worked for Ireland's main news analysis show, called *Prime Time* (think *60 Minutes*). His reaction to my blog post was interesting.

"Will you come on the show tonight? No one is saying what you are about the IFA salary scandal."

Fran's reaction shows the power of acting on your hunch—he connected directly with my intuition. This is what can happen when you act on a hunch. You directly wire into a new tone of voice that resonates with people. You are saying what they are thinking, and you are communicating from your Magic Slice.

Reaction 3—"I've Never Thought of This Before"

When you share something with your audience and they have the reaction "I've never thought of this before," then you've struck gold. You are in your Magic Slice, and you are there by being unique. Your message stands out and is experienced as something new, curious, and fresh.

But coming up with truly original ideas is very difficult, some might even say impossible. American writer Mark Twain once gave a stark assessment of the possibility of creating new ideas.

> There is no such thing as a new idea. It is impossible. We simply take a lot of old ideas and put them into a sort of mental kaleidoscope. We give them a turn and they make new and curious combinations. We keep on turning and making new combinations indefinitely; but they are the same old pieces of colored glass that have been in use through all the ages.[32]

SPANX

Sara Blakely single-handedly created the brand Spanx, an undergarment focused on delivering the perfect fit for women's clothes. In the process, she showed the power of audience targeting with a genuinely new idea. Her innovation, energy, doggedness, and drive for a new way to design and manufacture hosiery shaped the Magic Slice of Spanx and makes the brand a great example of the "I've never thought of this before" category.

Let's examine the Spanx brand story in Sara's own words. It illustrates how her energy and drive make the brand and, in turn, the brand story unique.

In 1998, Sara Blakely was twenty-seven years old and selling office equipment in Atlanta, Georgia, when she came up with the idea for Spanx. She wanted to feel more confident and comfortable in the clothes she wore. She recalls the moment she knew she was onto something: "I spent all my hard-earned money on this one pair of cream pants that hung there, and I decided to cut the feet out of control top pantyhose one day, and I threw them on under my white pants, and went to the party." The positive reactions Blakely received were instant. "I looked fabulous, I felt great, I had no panty lines, I looked thinner and smoother, but they rolled up my legs all night. And I remember thinking, 'This should exist for women.'"[33]

But the obstacles to her being the person to bring this unique product to the market were huge. She explains, "I'd never taken a business class, I'd never worked in fashion or retail. I'd actually been selling fax machines door-to-door for seven years since graduating from college, and I had $5,000 in savings. I'd just moved out of my mom's house, and I was dating a loser."[34]

Sara did what most people would do in that situation. She went to the internet. She looked up "hosiery mills." She got on the phone and started calling all of these hosiery mills to make a simple request: "Please help me make this idea of this footless, pantyhose-shaper concept."[35] And guess what? Everybody hung up the phone.

But Sara was a determined woman who believed in her new idea, and she wanted to protect it. She decided to patent it. She wanted to find a female patent attorney because she thought it would be much easier to explain her idea. She couldn't find one. Why? Because there wasn't a single female patent attorney in the whole state of Georgia. So she decided to write her own patent.

At the same time, she needed to find someone to turn her idea into a product. As she was writing her patent, she took a week off work to convince someone to make her idea. After a week of fruitless cold-calling, she returned home. Then, two weeks later, she got a call from one of the mill owners. He had asked his two daughters about it, and they thought it was a great idea.

And that set Blakely on a journey of trying to make the prototype. It took her a year of working on it at night and on the weekends. During that time, she learned so much that had never occurred to her as a consumer. She also learned that most undergarments were made by men who had little or no understanding of the issues women faced. She started testing prototypes on real women—her mom, her grandmother, all her friends.

She channeled uniqueness into every aspect of the product. The packaging was red with illustrations of women on it, which completely set it apart in the hosiery section. She even injected her uniqueness into the brand name Spanx by using a short word and an "x" to grab attention and make it memorable.

From the very first evening Sara Blakely wore Spanx, she channeled the audience reaction "I've never thought of this before." Her idea for Spanx was so far out that no one had genuinely considered it before. She put that feeling into everything she did, and she believed in it. It shaped her brand and how she communicates and is the essence of the Spanx Magic Slice. There is a lot to be learned from that.

Points to Ponder

- To know your Magic Slice and to be able to communicate from it, you need a deep understanding of your audiences.

- The audiences for your product or service are never static. Tastes, trends, and attitudes are in constant flux. As communicators, our job is to be a divining rod and constantly tune in to our audiences. Do you keep an audience file, or do you regularly check in on your audiences? If you don't, you should.

- Never forget the four audience questions you need to know:

  - How would you describe your audience in a sentence?

  - What are the defining traits of the people in your audience?

  - Who or what influences them?

  - What are their pain points and how do you cure them?

- It has never been easier to find out what your audience is feeling. There are a myriad of tools and techniques available. They include:

- Google Trends

- Online surveys

- Focus groups

- Social media questions

- SEO analytics

- Measuring how people are using your products and asking them why

- Net Promoter Score (a great way to find out exactly what customers think of your product)

Exercise for You

- Start by describing your product or service in a single sentence. This will focus you in on the customer.

- List all the defining traits of your ideal target customer. These are things that set your customers apart from others; someone who has these traits is part of your customer audience. They should include some of the following:

- Age

- Gender

- Hobbies or specific interests

- Location

- Disposable income

- Occupation

- What influences your customer audience? Write out a list of things that influence their decision-making.

- Write a paragraph describing one of your target customers in detail. Give them a name, age, and job title. Where do they live? What do they do for a living?

Step 3
Create Your Magic Slice Topics for Stories

Your Magic Slice Topics are what set your stories apart. These are the subject areas that you are naturally excellent at telling stories about and that resonate with your audience. Let's discover how to identify your Magic Slice Topics.

So what are your Magic Slice Topics? I want you to imagine a big folder in front of you, one of those large hardback ones you have in your office. This is the folder that documents your organization's Magic Slice.

Imagine it is jam-packed full of interesting stories about your organization and your work. Its title is "My Organisation's Amazing Stories."

Now imagine there are six dividers in the folder, each one clearly marked with a different story topic. What would these be for you? These topics should be unique to you and your story. They should give you definition and provide you with structure and inspiration in equal measure. Together, we will discover what your Magic Slice Topics are.

For example, if I ran a healthy bakery, my topics might be:

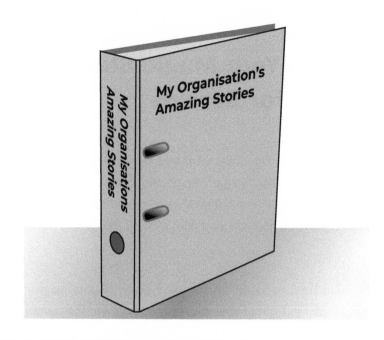

- Healthy bread recipes

- The history of brown bread

- Great ingredients

- The life of a pastry chef

- Bread of the week

- Sandwich porn (I know, a little weird, but imagine
  pictures of amazing sandwiches!)

At the end of this chapter, I will give you a specific
exercise to help you find your Magic Slice Topics.

What to Consider When Choosing Your Magic Slice Topics

What Are You Selling?

Everyone is selling something—what are you selling? What is your product or service, and can you describe it in a compelling way in a single sentence? This may not be as easy an exercise as it should be. If you are struggling here, you need to find clarity. Ask yourself what makes you different from your direct competitors and what your customers might substitute instead of choosing your product.

Be on the Right Side of the Zeitgeist

What are the biggest trends happening in your industry right now, and where do you stand on them? I am not talking about fads or passing fancies. I'm talking about structural, long-term changes in customer behavior. For example, in tourism, it could be a move toward sustainability and adventure holidays, or healthy-food breaks. In food, it could be a move away from plastic packaging and a need for more sustainable production.

What Do People Search For?

I am not a fountain of knowledge on search engine optimization, but I know that to truly understand an industry or a business, you need to know the key search terms. You should know the top twenty search terms people use when they want to find your product or service. You should be influenced by this, but don't be a slave to it. Anything that is too driven by search keywords is dry, boring, and easy to see through. The trick is to take the elements of these search terms and make sure they are integrated properly into your stories.

What Makes You Stand Apart from the Rest?

What makes your product or service unique? What sets it apart from the rest? Could you list three things?

Here are some examples:

- **Hoka**: There are hundreds of sneaker brands, but Hoka specializes in having extra cushion, and this has led to huge demand from people with joint pain.

- **Lush**: What makes Lush different from other cosmetic brands is handmade products. Its customers are committed to ethical buying and the purity of a handmade item.

- **Happy Socks**: Happy Socks is founded on the idea of being different from its competitors. Its mission is to spread happiness by turning socks—an everyday item of clothing—into a fashion statement. That's unique.

What Do You Value Most?

What does your organization value most? At MediaHQ, the media contacts company I founded, we value ingenuity, creativity, individuality, and curiosity. We look for these traits in new hires, and we work to deliver them in our software product.

Exemplary Storytelling: Hiut Denim

One good way to show you how to shape your Magic Slice topics is to tell you a story. It's the story of a denim jeans brand in a small town in West Wales called Hiut Denim.

It's one of my favorite stories, and it showcases everything that is good about storytelling and what we've been talking about up to this point.

David and Clare Hieatt believe in change, the environment, and doing one thing well. Their commitment to creativity, sustainability, and their local community in West Wales has created a much sought-after jeans brand with a difference.

David's a doer and an entrepreneur in the purest sense of the word. He grew up in the South Wales mining valleys, and from the start he was imbued with an independent spirit.

He was just three years old when he met Clare. She was eighteen months old, not long out of the cradle. She lived across the street from his cousin. They started dating when Clare was sixteen. They are both creative, but David is a dreamer, while Clare is more pragmatic. From the start, they were good for each other.

At just sixteen, David quit his A levels to set up his first "sportswear business" selling trainers (or sneakers) at a stall at Pontypridd Market. It taught him the importance of selling and why owning a good pair of shoes is a necessity. When he had a good day, he had enough money to buy petrol to get home. On a bad day, he walked. It was as simple as that. He was bitten by the bug. He recalls that time fondly. "I had borrowed £500 from my dad, which was most of his savings…Within six months, I had lost all his money."[36]

A few years later, David moved to London to become an advertising copywriter. At just twenty-one, his spark and flair were recognized when he joined the creative team at the acclaimed London advertising agency Saatchi & Saatchi. While there, he contributed to campaigns for British Airways and the Conservatives, under the mentorship of famed ad maverick Paul Arden.[37]

David had arrived at a place where his creative urge was satisfied every day, and he felt like he had joined the best club in the world, surrounded by people who loved ideas. At Saatchi, he learned to take risks and trust his gut. These are two traits that would reward him over and over again in his career.

Around this time, he first moved in with Clare. She had finished a degree in drama, and David encouraged her to consider a career as a copywriter. After completing a postgraduate course, she started work in an advertising agency. But she hated the London agency scene and became the in-house copywriter for the Body Shop at a great time for the brand. It gave Clare a deep understanding of the messages that work and resonate with ethical brands.

From his early days as a market trader, David's heart was set on sportswear, and he left Saatchi to follow the Adidas account to rival agency Leagas Delaney. But by the time he was offered a dream role with Adidas in 1995, he and Clare were already building their own clothing brand, Howies, from their living room floor. They started by making T-shirts, and David told everyone it was a hobby. It wasn't.

David's dad was their first shareholder. Along with the money, he gave them advice. "Wherever you go, go with all your heart."[38] With his words of advice ringing in their ears, they wrapped their whole philosophy and values about life into it. For six years, they did not pay themselves. The love of Howies kept them going.

They continued to work hard at their day jobs, but on Friday nights they pursued their dream: Howies. David shortened the life of the office photocopier by years as he printed the rough draft of what would become the Howies catalog.

By their midthirties, David and Clare had itchy feet and had grown tired of the hustle and bustle of London. Their daughter was just eighteen months old, and they fantasized about moving home to Wales. To motivate themselves, they made a poster and put it on the back of their bedroom door. The more they made a plan to leave, the more they realized that Howies was their ticket out of London. It presented them with an opportunity to create the life they wanted.

They found a farmhouse outside the coastal town of Cardigan in West Wales and were smitten. "With its rabble of outbuildings," this house had the space and wildness they were after, Clare recalled.[39]

Borrowing from their day jobs as copywriters, they created a phrase to describe their once-in-a-lifetime move. They saw themselves as "Big City Defectors." In the first few Howies catalogs after they moved, they told that story, and it began to resonate with people. The image of being able to canoe to work or grow organic vegetables resonated with people. David and Clare got their first taste of the power of the narrative in their own business. It became part of their Magic Slice.

Howies had grown from just T-shirts into an active sports clothing company whose deliciously subversive take on T-shirt design won it a cult following among mountain-biking, skateboarding, and surf-mad twentysomethings.

It was an upstart brand. Whatever Clare and David lacked in budget, they more than made up for in creativity and a bold approach. Bold, independent ideas became a huge part of their Magic Slice. David recalls the impact they had, always with a wry smile. "We got banned from The Mountain Bike Show, we got sued by Levis, we saw our favourite band wear our T-shirts, we argued with Banksy, we won awards, we got voted one of the best brands in the UK."[40]

The brand was growing fast, and David had dreams of being bigger than Nike. But by 2006, Howies was growing too fast and needed some more investment. The brand was riding high, and two companies wanted to invest. In the end, the couple decided to sell to Timberland as it understood the importance of Wales to the brand.

But it didn't work out, and the couple eventually left the business. David and Clare were never meant to be small cogs in a large company. There was too much loss of autonomy. David took the decision hard. "I also had to look at myself and ask some tough old questions. And the uncomfortable truth was, if I had been smarter at running a business, I never would have had to sell it to anybody. Looking back, I could see that I had learnt how to build a brand, but not how to run a business."[41]

They took time out to decide what to do next. David and Clare were a couple who would never be idle for too long. They started a new venture based on their obsession with purpose-driven work. They wanted to create a safe space to ask better questions. And they wanted to gather together makers, doers, and thinkers from all around the world in the old cowshed outside Cardigan to talk about getting things done and about changing the world. They called it the Do Lectures. It started with one hundred people, and it quickly grew into an event that is held in both Wales and California. Tickets are by application only, it sells out in a morning, and it has spawned a publishing company, Do Books, which publishes inspirational pocket guides for entrepreneurs and creative people.

After Howies, the Hieatts still felt they had unfinished business with building a clothing brand. They had learned many lessons, but the drive to grow, and to grow quickly, ultimately meant they lost control of their company. They learned bigger isn't always better. That lesson hurt David deeply, as he had driven their growth. They both wanted to put that lesson to use.

They had an idea about starting a jeans company. Jeans were always the bestsellers at Howies, and they were drawn to the item as a simple and classic utility product. They drew up a plan, but it lay on the shelf as they pondered what the purpose of their new business would be. It was a good plan, but why do it? The lesson they learned was that the "why" was the most important thing in business.

Then one day, out of the blue, David received a phone call from one of their former designers, Gideon, that changed everything. He wanted to know why they weren't doing the denim plan, because he loved it, and he told him they should manufacture locally and get Cardigan, their hometown, back to making jeans again. In that moment, they had worked out the "why."

The answer to their "why" had been under their noses all along. Cardigan is rooted in the craft of making jeans, even if it is, famously, also a type of sweater. It was once home to the biggest jeans factory in Britain, employing four hundred in a town of four thousand people. They made thirty-five thousand pairs of jeans every week.

Dewhirst Ladieswear had made jeans for Marks & Spencer until, in November 2002, it closed the Cardigan operation and moved production to Morocco. The shutdown was like a death, ripping the heart out of the town and putting 10 percent of the population out of work overnight.

The Hieatts recognized that, even though the factory was gone almost a decade, the skills remained embedded in their local community. "Even the postman who picks up our parcels at the end of the day used to cut jeans for 20 years," David told the *Guardian* newspaper. "Like humans, towns can lose confidence. Cardigan lost some of its mojo when Dewhirst closed. It was world-class at making jeans one day, and the next day it was gone. They [staff] have got a second chance, myself and Clare have got a second chance and so has the town," he added.[42]

So they took the first two letters of their surname, combined them with the first two letters in the word "utility," and Hiut Denim was born in 2011.

The years of experience building brands, telling stories, and tuning into purpose helped David and Clare arrive at the mission for Hiut Denim.

"We want to get our town making jeans again."

They started by hiring four of the workers from the Dewhirst factory, but this time it was going to be different. The machinists at Hiut Denim are called grandmasters because some of them have over forty years of experience making jeans. Each grandmaster does every job to complete a pair of jeans. It takes about one hour and twenty minutes to complete a single pair, and when they are finished, they sign each pair with a bright red marker. This production time compares to an average of eleven minutes for the highly industrialized jeans sector. The price is also different. Hiut commands a significant margin for their jeans, with prices ranging from £155 ($216) to £240 ($334).

At Hiut Denim, small details matter because every detail communicates a feeling to the customer. In addition to each grandmaster signing every pair of jeans they work on, there is considerable detail in the packaging. Jeans are folded and placed in a white inner bag, which is emblazoned with a photograph of a pair of jeans perfectly folded from one side to the other. This bag is then placed into a paper "potato" style bag and stitched closed.

When you look at Hiut Denim, the lessons learned from the sale of Howies to Timberland are everywhere. The Hieatts have remained in full control of the brand and sell directly to market via the internet. "Without the internet, we'd have been dead within 12 weeks," David told the BBC in 2017. "But the internet has changed only everything. The internet allows us to sell direct and keep the [profit] margin...it enables us to compete."[43]

But what has also been invaluable is the Hieatts' ability to tell a great story and shape the Magic Slice of the brand—a skill learned over years of dedicated practice.

In my assessment, Hiut Denim's Magic Slice Topics are:

- **Makers**: the craft of makers, their workshops, and manufacturing in the UK

- **Creativity**: the power of handmade things

- **Sustainability**: making things that last

- **Continuous improvement**: getting 1 percent better every day

- **Focus**: so they do one thing well

- **Community**: the story of their town making jeans again

- **The old ways**: investing time to learn a craft and sharing that with others

Their storytelling has enabled them to tell the Hiut Denim story effectively on many different platforms, from the company's sharp brand website and engaging blog to its extensive use of social media, with advertisements in people's Facebook feeds and arty photos of people wearing its jeans. Storytelling has played a huge part in helping Hiut Denim reach "geeks" in the hipster hotspots of London, New York, and Tokyo.

The brand has gained influential devotees, including Meghan Markle, the aging punks the Stranglers, and Ant and Dec, who wore the Welsh company's jeans during *I'm a Celebrity*. The TV presenters also gave the jeans-maker an unexpected boost by tweeting their denim allegiance to their millions of followers. The plug was invaluable, David says. "Celebrities have an incredible power, and when your marketing budget is as big as your coffee budget, it's great because we couldn't afford to reach those people by traditional means."[44]

"The interesting thing about social media for me is that up until Facebook, Instagram, Twitter, and Snapchat you had to have a huge budget in order to tell your story," he says.[45]

"In effect, you were locked out of telling that story because the costs [of advertising and wider marketing] were too high. But social media has actually allowed the smaller maker [a small firm that manufactures things] to go and tell his story," he adds.[46]

Other marketing initiatives that have given the brand an impact far beyond its small budget include the brand catalog, which is almost a work of art, and its blog, which celebrates makers from all over the world. David is never short of ideas, and over the years, the brand has introduced a history tag to document who has worn a pair of jeans and an initiative to get super users to "break in" a pair of jeans for six months without washing and send them back to the factory for sale.

Since they started Hiut Denim in 2011, David and Clare have built a strong and profitable brand, and they've got the people of Cardigan back to making jeans again. Their success is built on their great partnership, their commitment to an independent life, and their ability to tell a great story. In 2018, the Hiut brand mission made a massive leap forward when, due to increasing sales, Hiut Denim moved its manufacturing into the old Dewhirst factory. The couple won't rest until they get their town back making jeans again.

Your challenge now is to define your own Magic Slice Topics. Here are some points to ponder before the specific set of exercises to help you.

Points to Ponder

- Do you understand how the Magic Slice is structured? Do you have all the elements that are required?

- Visualize the folder called "My Organization's Amazing Stories," and imagine what the six dividers would be titled. This really focuses the mind and what you need to do.

- As someone who is leading storytelling in your organization, you should act as a divining rod for the Magic Slice. This means you should have an innate understanding of the industry you are in and an affinity with your customers.

- You are looking for four to six topics that define your organization and set it apart from your competitors. It is not about fitting in; it's about standing out.

- If you know your own mind, finding your Magic Slice will be easier. Everything becomes clearer when you know how you'd like to be defined by others.

Exercises for You

It's time to find the Magic Slice Topics for your brand or organization.

The common pitfall with specifying topics is that people make them too narrow. Remember, they are like dividers in a large folder. Look at how broad and enabling Hiut Denim's Magic Slice Topics are. One of Virgin's is simply its founder, Richard Branson, articulated with one word: Richard. You can see the possibilities of this and how it almost suggests stories. One of clothing brand Patagonia's is environmental activism.

- What is your product or service? It's not complicated. Describe it in a single sentence.

- Tell me three exciting trends or things that are happening in your industry right now.

- Tell me three things that make your brand or organization different or unique. In the example of Hiut Denim, this included "handmade" and "locally manufactured."

- What are the things you value most in how you deliver your service? If you are stuck, think of the qualities you would really love in your next hire. These are the things you value.

- Revisit your mission and your foundation story from Step 1. Use those and the answers you have to the questions here to decide on between four and six Magic Slice Topics.

Step 4
Create Your Magic Slice Statement

Your Magic Slice Statement. It is a powerful paragraph that simply conveys the essence of your Magic Slice. It is a short description unique to you that describes your mission, your target customer, what sets you apart, and the topics your stories are about.

You've done all the hard work; now it's time to articulate your Magic Slice Statement.

You can't truly adopt storytelling as a way to communicate unless you ground it in the center of your organization and you consistently tell stories about the topics and themes that truly resonate with your audiences.

It can be daunting to change how you communicate, but let's pause for a moment to see exactly where we are in figuring out your Magic Slice. Take a look at the graphic below. It outlines the shape of the journey you need to take to discover your Magic Slice.

Great storytelling brands like Virgin, Patagonia, and Blendtec instinctively follow this structure. They have a strong foundation story and a compelling mission statement, and they bring these to life with stories in how they communicate every day.

In this chapter, you are first going to write a short Magic Slice Statement. Step 5, which we will get to next, will be to write individual stories under each topic area.

Remember, the process of communicating with stories is dynamic, with each element affecting the others. It also means you can revisit any element of your Magic Slice. But any change should be translated into a change in how you communicate.

The higher up the change you make in the Magic Slice process, the more profound the change will be. For example, if you change your organization's mission or a fundamental aspect of your foundation story, then this should be reflected in your Magic Slice Statement and in your topics.

Red Bull

The brand Red Bull is a really good example of this change. Today, Red Bull is a global media company and an energy drink associated with extreme sports, but it started life with a very different story. It changed the Magic Slice of its brand by changing its mission.

In 1976, Chinese entrepreneur Chaleo Yoovidhya introduced a new drink in Thailand called Krating Daeng, which means "red gaur" or "Indian bison" in English. It was inspired by the tonic Lipovitan, the prime ingredient of which is taurine.[47]

In Thailand, energy drinks are popular among low-paid workers who endure long hours: taxi, tuk-tuk, truck, and bus drivers and construction workers. Workers like fifty-three-year-old Phakhaphon Kheamthong, whose life is so typical of this group. His job as a motorcycle taxi driver means "spending 12 hours a day, six days a week navigating the congested streets of central Bangkok in muggy tropical heat and a haze of exhaust fumes." Whenever he feels exhausted, which you can imagine is regularly, he uses a pick-me-up, which "comes from a small 150ml amber glass bottle [Krating Daeng] that looks like it was bought from a pharmacy."[48]

In 1982, Austrian entrepreneur Dietrich Mateschitz visited Thailand and discovered that Krating Daeng magically helped cure his jet lag. He saw something different in a product that was almost solely used by low-paid workers to give them something extra to keep toiling away.

Instead of a drink, he saw a source of energy and thought it was a valuable commodity. He wanted to create a new brand with a different story.

Two years later, in 1984, Mateschitz co-founded Red Bull GmbH with Yoovidhya and began turning it into the global brand we know today. They changed the focus of the product away from low-paid workers and started to recreate it as an energy drink.

They began sponsoring extreme events. The slogan "Red Bull gives you wings" was born, and humor and cartoons became a central part of how they told the story.

They kept the product, but they changed everything else. They changed its mission, its target audience, and the brand's Magic Slice.

Your Magic Slice Progress

Let's get to work and identify all the storytelling elements we already have and the ones we need to get.

- A new, revised **foundation story** for your organization that is authentic to who you are and what you do. You completed this exercise at the end of the "What Is a Story?" chapter of the book.

- A compelling **mission statement** that you bring to life every day, which motivates your customers, your staff, and your suppliers. This was completed at the end of the "Find a Mission and Articulate It" part of the book.

- In Step 2, you identified your audiences.

- In Step 3, you completed your Magic Slice Topics.

We will use all of this information to shape your Magic Slice Statement.

Hiut Denim

We took a deep look at the story behind Hiut Denim. Let's look at the different elements of its Magic Slice.

- **Mission**: to get its town of Cardigan back to making jeans again

- **What does it do?** Makes beautiful handcrafted jeans

- **Target customer**: a discerning and creative person who values the craft and quality of handmade things

- **Magic Slice Topics**: making, creativity, community, focus, self-improvement, and independence

Based on this information, this is how I would shape Hiut Denim's Magic Slice Statement:

Hiut Denim's mission is to get its town of Cardigan back making jeans again. It believes in the power of doing one thing well—that's why it makes only jeans. Its target customer is a discerning and creative person who values the craft and quality of handmade things. Its stories are about making, creativity, community, focus, self-improvement, and independence.

Bandcamp

Another good example is the website Bandcamp, which was set up in 2008 to give musicians and artists greater control of their work and allow them to earn more royalties. Let's look at the different elements that make up its Magic Slice.

- **Mission**: to help spread the healing power of music by building a community where artists thrive through the direct support of their fans and where fans gather to explore the amazing musical universe that their direct support helps create

- **What does it do?** Operates an online record store and music community

- **Target customer**: musicians, artists, and their passionate fans who want to discover, connect with, and directly support the artists they love

- **Magic Slice Topics**: new artists, new music releases, featured artists, playlists, artist interviews

Based on this, here is how I would shape Bandcamp's Magic Slice Statement:

> Bandcamp runs an online record store and vibrant music and artistic community. Its mission is to help spread the healing power of music by building a community where artists thrive through the direct support of their fans and where fans gather to explore the amazing musical universe their direct support helps create. It exists to serve musicians, artists, and their passionate fans who want to discover, connect with, and directly support the artists they love. They tell stories about new artists, new music releases, cultural trends, and curated sounds.

Canva

Canva is a software tool that was founded in 2012 to help make publishing and design easier. Here are the elements of its Magic Slice:

- **Mission**: to empower everyone in the world to design anything and publish anywhere

- **What does it do?** It provides an online design and publishing tool. It believes in making complex things simple, being a force for good, empowering others, and setting big crazy goals and making them happen.

- **Target customer**: business owners, marketeers, and professionals not versed in design

- **Magic Slice Topics**: business, design inspiration, design elements and principles, creativity, branding

This is how I think its Magic Slice Statement might read:

Canva is an online publishing and design platform. Its mission is to empower everyone in the world to design anything and publish anywhere. It is driven to make complex things simple, be a force for good, empower others, and set big crazy goals and make them happen. It serves business owners, marketeers, and professional people not trained in design. Its stories are about business, design inspiration, and design elements and principles.

Your challenge is to write your own Magic Slice Statement. Here are some points to ponder before a specific exercise to help you.

Points to Ponder

- Do you understand how the Magic Slice is structured?

- Do you have all the required elements, and are you happy with them?

- Make sure your statement captures the essence of who you are and gives you space to grow.

Exercises for You

Writing your Magic Slice Statement at this stage should be a simple editing exercise. It should be a brief paragraph and should draw from all the elements in the Magic Slice structure.

It's a single paragraph that includes mission, values, target customer audience, and topics. Have a go at writing your Magic Slice Statement. Start by:

- Writing down your mission statement

- Writing down a description of your target customer

- Writing down what makes you unique and the things that you value

- Listing your Magic Slice Topics

When you have all of these elements, blend them into a paragraph. Hone it to make it flow. Remember, less is always more.

Step 5
Generate Compelling Stories

To be able to communicate with stories, you have to be able to generate enough good ideas that fit with your Magic Slice Topics. But that is not enough. You also have to be able to shape these ideas into compelling stories that resonate with your audience. Let's explore how to do this.

We've arrived at the place where you come up with great stories for your brand. The funny thing is that this is the place where most people want to start, without doing any of the hard work you have done. No mission, no foundation story, no audience analysis, no Magic Slice; they just want to lash out the stories. And guess what? That approach doesn't work. Yes, it might have sporadic success, and it might be okay for a while, but it will quickly run out of steam.

The good news is that if you've reached this point in the book, you've done the hard work. You've designed your own story machine; our job now is to get it working.

In the graphic below you can see that we start with the Magic Slice Topic and work our ideas out of that topic. This way, we are ensuring your stories are completely plugged into your brand or your organization.

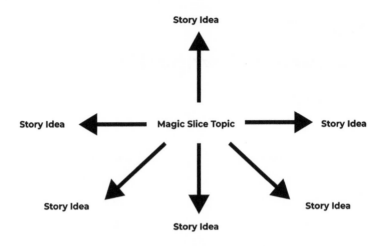

How Hiut Denim Does It

Let's look at what this looks like for an example from Hiut Denim. One of its Magic Slice Topics is being "1% better." Here's what it looks like when you use the Magic Slice Story Idea Map to expand six stories out of it.

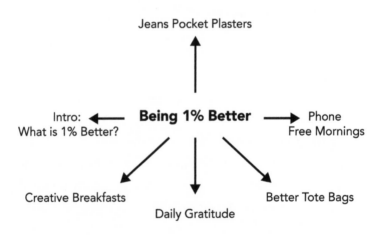

Let's look at the topic in detail. Every couple of years, Hiut Denim produces its high-quality yearbook. It commissions original photography, poetry, design, and stories. It has great business writers like Seth Godin to write for it. How does it do this? By having a great idea, and just by asking. You'd be amazed how powerful that can be.

It's called the yearbook, but it's actually the catalog—a showcase for the brand. It's such a high-quality production that the company charges for it. Isn't that mad and more than a little audacious? The theme for its fifth yearbook was "One percent better."

On its blog, it has a Magic Slice Topic entitled "One percent better." Here's how it is described:

Let's begin.

Here's the question this Yearbook asks.

How can I get better today than I was yesterday?

Most people ignore the small things they can do because they don't offer a big or fast enough result. Instead, they seek to attempt to hit the ball out of the park. Take the big swing. Go for glory.

Big wins are rare. Small wins are common. *They happen every day.* Yup, the power of the incremental gain over time provides a much better result.

The compounding effect of trying to get better by 1% a day is enormous. Compounded it is 3,800%

per year. That's almost 40 times better than where you started in just one year.

Over the next 100 days, we will document our small wins. And then put them all in our yearbook. We hope it becomes a manifesto for the small win. If it does, that will be a big win. *So, here goes.*[49]

It is interesting to observe how open and transparent the process is. It sets its Magic Slice Topic and says it is going to blog one hundred stories about it. Each story is about an improvement in how it performs. At the end of the process, it logs all the stories about improvements in a book it sells.

It's worth noting Hiut Denim's house style for writing stories. They tend to be short, punchy, often lyrical, and quite sparse. They can be almost like poetry. They come from David and Clare's years as successful copywriters. They are experts at sharing individual stories that lift the lid on what they do and sharing their processes. Every story adds another element to the brand's capital. It's not a style that would work for every brand, but it is who they are, and because of that, it's authentic.

Let's take a deeper look at some of the individual stories behind the Magic Slice Topic "1 percent better":

Jeans Plaster Pockets

This is a story asking why every jeans company makes a jean with a pocket card stitched to it when you buy it. Post purchase, it only stays on there for a few moments. In this story, the company asks, How could Hiut Denim make this feature of the product better? To solve this problem, it decided to look to two of its other values: great design and a sense of purpose. It added photographs to the cards and turned them into a reminder of its "No Wash Club," an incentive to get its users not to wash the jeans for six months.

Phone-Free Mornings

This is a short story about the power of smartphones to distract and limit that most valuable of commodities: focus. The story encourages people to create a culture where they step back for a morning to break a bad habit and create a good one.

Better Tote Bags

This is a story about tote bags, which are much-desired pieces of merchandise, especially among Hiut Denim's hipster clientele. In this story, it talks about the design of its tote bags, which hasn't changed for eight years. Its tote bag has an image of the firm's logo of an owl, but addressing the customer directly, Hiut Denim contends that this is too much about the company and not enough about the customer. It tried to change to a tote bag that said "Stay Weird" but openly admitted it was a poor attempt. It asked designer James Victore to bring the Stay Weird tote bag to life, and he recreated it with a special card. It also changed the material to organic cotton.

Creative Breakfasts

Every week, the staff at Hiut Denim arrives early, drinks good coffee, and eats croissants. Everyone shares their best inspiration from the week. It's a fun time with laughter and shaping a new worldview. It creates motivation and builds a culture of creativity.

Daily Gratitude

This is a story about the power of saying thanks for the small things. Things like questions, constraints, barriers, curveballs, small budgets, and the status quo. It is a classic Hiut Denim story. It is sparse, inspirational, and thought-provoking. In storytelling terms, there is not an ounce of fat on it. It does exactly what it's supposed to do.

The Floyd Leg—Furniture with a Story

Another example of a brand that is great at storytelling from its Magic Slice is Floyd, a Detroit furniture company started in 2016 by Kyle Hoff and Alex O'Dell with a Kickstarter campaign. It set a goal to raise $18,000 for a simple new furniture idea: a set of steel screw-on legs that could turn any flat surface into a table.

It didn't just ask for the money: it told a story. The idea started when O'Dell wanted a new table for his apartment but didn't want to have to buy a bulky piece of furniture, because he moved around all the time. The company wanted to make furniture that was reusable and kind to the environment, a reaction to the disposable IKEA culture. Its Kickstarter investment pitch was focused on creative people, millennials, and those who valued sustainability.

They called the company Floyd in homage to O'Dell's dad, grandfather, and great-grandfather—all called Floyd, and all steel mill workers. It set up in Detroit, which was going through a massive regeneration after decades in decline and got local machine shops to do all its manufacturing.

The story worked and its Kickstarter raised a phenomenal $256,273, some 1,400 percent of what it was looking for. It was off to a great start. Since then, it has added a number of innovative products based on the same design philosophy and values, including a bed frame, a sofa, a shelving system, and a table. I was so taken by its story that I ordered a set of the Floyd legs for my new conference room in 2017 and told its story during every Magic Slice strategy session I gave.

The way it communicates has evolved since 2016. Its Magic Slice now has three topics:

Learn

This is where it shares two things:

- Its sustainability mission

- Its focus on great design

Lived In

It shares stories of its product in action. These include reviews of homes, product reviews, interior advice, and interviews about its approach to making new products.

Stay Floyd

This is a collaboration with Airbnb where you can stay in Airbnb properties that have Floyd products. They are full of beautiful pictures of amazing homes and transport you to another way of living.

Let's look in detail at what the stories in the Lived In Magic Slice look like.

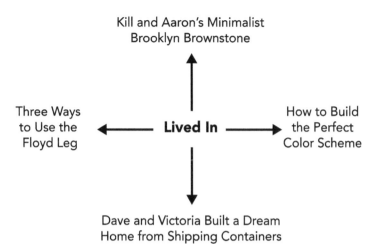

Writing Your Own Stories

Here are some things to consider when writing your stories.

1. Tune In to Other Brands

Above, we looked at how Hiut Denim and Floyd each execute their Magic Slice. With the knowledge you are now armed with about the process, you should look at how other brands do it. Tune in to the overall story approach and then look specifically at how they execute individual stories. You will learn a lot.

2. Remember the Rules

In Part 1, we looked at the three distinct areas of a story—don't forget them. They are:

- The elements

- The structure

- The form

It is essential for you to understand each one and apply it to your stories.

3. Don't Get Hung Up on Form

One of the common pitfalls in storytelling is that people get obsessed about the form a story takes. They say things like "We need to do a Facebook or Instagram post." By doing this, you will miss what's really important. Every good idea has to survive in written form first. If it's not compelling on the page in words, it won't work in another form, like video, audio, or social media. Commit your idea to paper, and only when you're sure it's good enough, think about the form.

4. Good Writing Is Essential

To have compelling stories people will want to read, the writing needs to be good. This is a common pitfall when brands and organizations communicate with stories—the quality of execution lets them down. It is essential that you work with good writers. It is also important that you develop a house style early on. I call this doing it "Johnny Cash style," from his song "One Piece at a Time." At the start, you should be doing this slowly.

5. Optimize for Search

I previously mentioned the importance of search engine optimization (SEO) in the chapter on audiences. It's essential to find a balance when it comes to having your story optimized for search. Trust me, if the search specialists had their way, your story would die under the weight of their requirements and everything would become clickbait. I am not a search expert, but I know it's important to know how to make your story more searchable. You should know the top searched terms in your industry and endeavor to include them as organically as you can. Your challenge is to do this without making what could be a great story into marketing drivel. It's achievable, but it will take some thought.

Never let good SEO ruin a good story.

Make that a rule.

6. Raw Idea + Headline = Story

This is an important equation. Just because you have a raw idea for a story doesn't mean you have a story. Let me give you an example. I once got a call from an academic who wanted to use MediaHQ to issue a press release. I asked him what the story's headline was. He told me it was:

"Have You Ever Heard about an Anti-memory?"

I was really confused and had no idea what the story was about. When I probed a little further, he told me he was studying the science behind the phenomenon of psychics. Let's look at the equation for his story.

> **Raw idea**: A new scientific study into psychics
> +
> **Headline**: New research study reveals the science behind psychics
> = **Story**

A number of years ago, I worked with forklift company Combilift on its story strategy as it expanded an old chicken factory into its new global headquarters.

> **Raw idea**: Forklift manufacturer moves into old chicken factory as new headquarters
> +
> **Headline**: €15 million ($18 million) investment in new global headquarters will see the creation of two hundred jobs by Combilift
> = **Story**

Here are the steps you should follow:

1. Start with raw ideas. Think of as many as you can. Then whittle them down to the best six or seven.

2. Write down one of these, and then write as many headlines as you can think of and pick the best one. Do this for each of the raw ideas.

3. Don't write any of the stories until you have the headline first. Too much energy is wasted on writing stories based on poorly thought-out ideas. A headline is like a call to action. The story should write itself.

Points to Ponder

- Before you even start coming up with a story idea, your fundamentals must be correct. Do you have a good foundation or origin story and a clear, compelling mission statement? Do you have a Magic Slice Statement and a set of Magic Slice Topics?

- A raw idea for a story is not a story; it's a raw idea for a story! It needs work to make it work. Remember, it needs a hook to make it a compelling story.

- Remember the story rules: a great story needs the right elements and structure—it is only then that you decide on the form.

- Great Magic Slice Topics can produce thousands of stories, so be creative.

- Don't just talk about your product; talk about the future of your industry and trends. Interview people and put personality at the heart of it.

Exercises for You

Generating Story Ideas from Your Categories

It's your turn to come up with ideas for one of your Magic Slice Topics.

Think of your six topics as the branches of a tree, and the sprouting leaves are your story ideas.

1. Refer to the six Magic Slice Topics you have decided on.

2. Choose one topic to start with, and think of all the story ideas that fit under that topic. You can use this diagram to make it easy. Write as many ideas as you can—don't limit yourself.

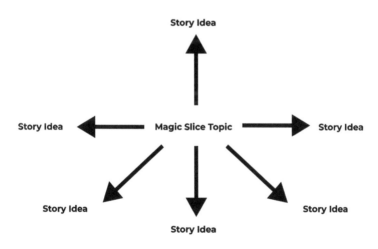

3. Draw it out like this in your notebook:

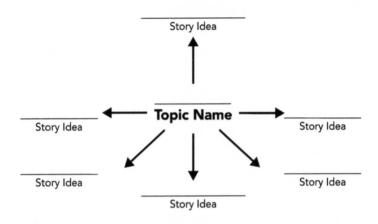

4. Take each story idea and write as many headlines for it as you can. Pick the best one. Here is an example of the format to use:

Story Idea: _____

Suggested Headlines:

- _____

- _____

- _____

- _____

- _____

- _____

- _____

- _____

- _____

- _____

5. Once you have a good headline, write the story. Don't forget to include the elements and how to structure the story.

6. Continue this process for each of the six topics.

7. Well done! Your story machine is now working.

This process doesn't necessarily have an endpoint. I would suggest six story ideas for each topic to begin with, but if your creative juices are flowing, why stop there?

Step 6
Revise and Edit Your Stories in the Light of Experience and the Changing Environment

Devising your Magic Slice is a process, and like all good processes, it should keep on running. Once you have completed your Magic Slice Statement and Topics, you should use them to generate stories. Then you should assess the Magic Slice Statement's effectiveness and tweak and change it as you need to.

This means you should use this framework every day to evaluate how you tell stories. The important thing is that you are continually tuned in to your Magic Slice. All of the items in the process can change at any stage, and you need to reflect these changes in how you tell stories.

Let's recap the process:

- **Step 1—Find a Mission and Articulate It**

  - **Your action point**: to have a mission statement you are proud of that is specific to you and that motivates your team, your customers, and your community

- **Step 2—Tune In to Your Different Audiences**

  - **Your action point**: written briefs that specifically describe your different target audiences and are a way to consistently tune in to their traits, needs, desires, and behaviors

- **Step 3—Create Your Magic Slice Topics for Stories**

  - **Your action point**: a written list of at least five distinct topics that act as a platform to tell your brand story

- **Step 4—Create Your Magic Slice Statement**

  - **Your action point**: a written Magic Slice Statement

- **Step 5—Generate Compelling Stories**

  - **Your action point**: a collection of distinct and well-written stories that tune your audience in to what is great about your brand or organization

- **Step 6—Revise and Edit Your Stories in the Light of Experience and the Changing Environment**

- **Your action point**: continually revisit this process, with the motivation to consistently make each element sharper, clearer, and more focused

***

You can revisit and edit any element of your Magic Slice at any time. It is important if you change any aspect of it that the change is reflected in how you tell stories. The higher up the change, the more fundamentally the change will be felt. Obviously, if you change your mission, then everything will change. However, if you launch a new product line or service, you might just acquire a new Magic Slice Topic.

Points to Ponder

- Telling stories that your audience wants to hear is essential. That's why you need to invest time and energy into discovering your Magic Slice.

- Do you have a compelling enough mission? Can you articulate it easily? Does it make you happy, excited, or even proud? If it doesn't, you need to work on it.

- Do you understand your audiences on a deep level? If not, what about them do you need to find out? Unless you understand who you are talking to, you will never become a great storyteller.

- What topics can you talk about that would really set you apart from your competitors? How can you be fresh, engaging, and interesting in how you communicate? You need to discover this to be a success.

- Are you or one of your team able to write great individual stories that will connect with people? What do these stories look like, and what do you need to do to be able to write them?

3

Putting Storytelling to Work for You

You are a storyteller. Take responsibility for how you communicate.

Tell a Story Every Chance You Get

Well done: you are now at the last stage of the Magic Slice journey.

In the first two parts of the book, we looked at how stories work, and if you have followed the exercises you will:

- Have a deep understanding of the power of story-telling as a communications tool

- Know the science behind how stories work

- Understand how to light your creative spark

- Have a compelling mission

- Know the elements and structure of a story and the different forms they take

- Know your Magic Slice Statement and Topics

- Have a list of great ideas for stories

But the last remaining question is probably one of the most important:

Where and When Do You Tell Your Stories?

It is one thing to know how to tell a story, but it only becomes an effective way to communicate when you know where and when to do it. Successful storytelling depends on the context in which the story is told.

During the storyteller courses I teach, I often encounter people who are amazing storytellers—except, that is, at work. They can be the life and soul of the party with their friends, but when they go to work, they become a corporate drone, devoid of their natural color, personality, and emotion. Once they are thinking in "work mode," all of their storytelling flair vanishes.

Storytelling won't happen because you think about it; you've got to act on it.

Storytelling is a *way*, not a *thing*; its energy should constantly flow through your organization. Like eating healthily or doing regular exercise, it will only get easier and more natural the more you practice it.

The first step in achieving your potential as a storyteller is to take personal responsibility. This is often the hardest step, because you may have to change how you think, build your confidence, or change how you work. Consider these two examples of how a great story makes the difference:

1. Startup

Every startup founder has an idea, an instinct, funding (maybe), and a story. It's the story that will separate the bland ideas from the businesses that really stand out. A story will take a raw idea and make it sing. If the dry workings of a business are the prose, then the story is the poetry. It's what raises the curiosity and gets people talking.

2. Starting a New Job or Project

If you are starting a new job or working on a new project, you will have an idea, the collective will of your team to succeed, and the story that binds you all together. If the story is good, then everything the team does will be clearer; if it is confusing, then confusion will take hold from the start and dictate everything.

You know that telling great stories from your Magic Slice will set you apart, but the responsibility to tell stories is yours, and you've got to own it. Unless you actively choose storytelling as the way you want to communicate, it won't happen. Storytelling won't happen simply by thinking about it; you've got to act on it. Imagine how powerful it will be when you not only know your Magic Slice but also know how and where to articulate it.

In the final part of the book, we will examine where and when you can fill your life with storytelling to have impact. We will do this by looking at a number of case studies of storytelling in action.

We will delve into:

- **Storytelling culture**: the practical steps you need to take to create a culture of storytelling in your organization, and what you can learn from Amazon

- **Public speaking**: how you can master public speaking and become a storyteller instead of a PowerPoint bore

- **Brand newsroom**: how to use a brand newsroom to execute your Magic Slice and your storytelling, and what you can learn from Marriott Hotels, Hackney Council, and Intercom

- **Glossary of Storytelling Tools**: a glossary of the practical tools

Everyone should be communicating with stories, not just the communications team.

How to Create a Culture of Storytelling

Organizations that naturally communicate with stories have that instinct hardwired into everything they do. When they are faced with a challenge, they meet it head-on with a story. They have what is called a *story-driven culture*.

Having a story-driven culture means you have created an environment within your organization that enables stories to naturally thrive.

Within this culture:

- Stories are encouraged as the natural response to any situation.

- People are empowered and rewarded to communicate with stories.

- The mission, values, and Magic Slice are understood.

- An apprentice ethos enables employees to learn story skills on the job.

Political parties have, by design, a story-driven culture. It's not the best candidate who wins an election; it's the one with the best story. I remember my time working on a political press team as a "university of storytelling" with each new crisis or triumph. It was a laboratory to test my storytelling skills.

In organizations with a story-driven culture, the Magic Slice is known and understood on a deep level, and everyone knows how to improvise with not just stories, but stories that are in their Magic Slice.

Throughout this book, we have mentioned and examined many organizations that have a story culture, each for a different reason:

- **Ryanair** has an insanely simple business proposition and a campaigning CEO in Michael O'Leary.

- **Spanx** is driven by the startup energy and creative spark of founder Sara Blakely.

- **Paddy Power's** story culture is realized through its mischief department. Its role is to deliver story opportunities that perfectly fit the brand's Magic Slice.

As you can see, there are many ways to foster a story culture in your organization. Here are five I recommend:

1. Make Everyone a Spokesperson for Your Organization

Who best understands the mission you are trying to achieve? It should be your customers, but it is most likely your staff. They work on the small details of what you deliver: the meetings, the quarterly plans, and the new ideas.

Why, then, do most organizations find it difficult to have even one person skilled enough to represent them in public? Imagine if everyone in your organization was capable of representing you in a live television interview. **Charity: water** is a great example of a brand with a story culture. Here is the story from its website about how Scott Harrison founded the charity:

> "After a decade of indulging his darkest vices as a nightclub promoter, Scott declared spiritual, moral, and emotional bankruptcy. He spent two years on a hospital ship off the coast of Liberia, saw the effects of dirty water first-hand, and came back to New York City on a mission."[50]

Like all great stories, it is to the point and reels you in. Everything Charity: water does is driven by story. It has created an army of advocates for its mission to deliver clean drinking water by training its staff and volunteers to tell the organization's story. And, importantly, it has made its army accessible to the world. On the corporate website, you can book a Charity: water spokesperson to speak at your conference or event.

To create an army of spokespeople, you need to resource your team by training them regularly in the skills of storytelling and ensuring they get the practice they need to excel.

2. Throw Away the Template

Corporate slide templates are a curse. They act like a straitjacket to confine creativity and limit personality. Have you ever wondered why the marketing department insists that every one of your slides has to look the same and have a logo in the corner? Templates are their way of marking their territory, like a dog peeing on a lamppost. Why does every square inch of a presentation have to be about the corporate brand? Believe me, if you told a great story that wasn't part of the template, the sky wouldn't fall in.

If you work in a large corporate environment, one way around the template in a presentation is to go off script by telling a story. Decide how you want to get the audience to *feel* and what the best story is to get them there. Your story will connect far better than any of the template slides.

Take pride in how your slides look. Most people aren't designers, but they know the difference between what looks good and what looks poor. A simple, pithy, tweetable phrase in black on a colored background will always work. A picture with nothing else also works. Study the imagery and slides used by great speakers that you like. Also make sure you use the same font throughout; consistency is important. And avoid clip art.

3. Make Telling a Story the Rule

A good way to foster a culture of storytelling is to ensure people tell stories at meetings. The easiest way to do this is to make this rule:

Bad PowerPoint is banned.

I'm a fan of using slide presentations the right way, with pictures and large, simple points, but too often they are used as a crutch for people to read things out loud. Imagine the change if your colleagues were banned from sharing slides full of bullet points. This cycle of boredom and frustration would stop instantly.

Storytelling is a way, not a thing.

Once, an enthusiastic attendee on a storyteller course interrupted me to ask a question. He'd been listening intently and applying the new techniques he was learning, but I knew he'd hit a wall by his confused look.

"This 'story way' of communicating is fine, but when my colleagues want a copy of my slides, they will be no good to them. They'll be just a random collection of images, words, and phrases. I'd be better giving them my family's holiday pictures than the slides."

When I probed his question, he said that before the course, his slides resembled a typed document with bullet points and he read them out loud at meetings. He was effectively running his senior management meetings like a kindergarten class. After he described this process out loud, I knew he realized how foolish it was.

"Surely your colleagues are not illiterate?" I asked, a little in jest. He assured me, with a smile, they were not. I pointed out that what they were engaged in was an act of madness.

"Wouldn't you be much better off forgetting the slides and sending your colleagues a briefing note before the meeting? Then you could have a proper discussion on the day of the meeting." Consider how making a change like this would improve the quality of everyone's life at work.

4. Practice Storytelling All the Time

How much practice do the people in your organization have to tell stories? When there is a presentation opportunity, is the limelight taken up by the same people, or is it shared?

One way to change your culture is by giving a voice to your team members. You can do this by insisting that everyone needs to play a part in presentations, not just the team leader or "the communicator" in the group.

Another way to foster the story spark in everyone is to make it fun. My company, MediaHQ, regularly gets our team members to make presentations on away days to entertain ourselves. It always introduces a nice frisson into the day. People get to talk about something they are passionate about, and it isn't work. It's a great way for people to communicate naturally as themselves and always creates empathy and a bond in a group.

5. Wrap Everything in Stories

Always start with the question, How could we tell a story about that? The old way to communicate was a polished launch and a shiny press release. The new way is to tell the story about the messy journey and pause at every step to share as much detail as you can.

Pat Phelan is a serial entrepreneur and the founder of SISU, a doctor-led clinic focused on aesthetics. He is also a master of social media, and as the SISU brand grows worldwide, he shares every small bit of detail as a story across all of his social channels. It could be a new location, a product launch, or something about the growth of the business—he makes everything a story, and all of his followers help him grow his brand.

Patrick Campbell is the CEO and founder of revenue operations software ProfitWell. He is so driven by stories, he created a unique experience when ProfitWell participated in SaaStock, the annual global showcase for his industry.

At the ProfitWell stand, it runs a mini-conference, almost like an event within an event. The stand has a small stage and its own café. Those who drop by get a free coffee from the barista and then sit down to drink it while they listen to one of the ProfitWell speakers. How could you wrap stories around everything you do?

To finish this chapter, I want to focus on a case study that highlights the transformative power of a storytelling culture on company performance. Let's take a closer look at the role of storytelling in the success of Amazon.

Amazon

Amazon is one of the largest and most dynamic companies the world has seen. Over the last ten years, its phenomenal growth has been fueled by a focus on the customer and innovation.

Jeff Bezos started selling books online long before he developed the idea for the "Everything Store." Since 2012, the company's exponential growth has seen greater scrutiny of its labor policies, benefits, working conditions, and practices.

During this time, there has also been an even greater interest in the factors that have made Amazon so successful. One part of the success that stands out is how Amazon makes decisions. It uses a method powered by stories that drives innovation and bold, clear decision-making. Let's discover how it does it.

On June 9, 2004, sometime before 6:00 p.m., Jeff Bezos sat down to write an email to his senior leadership team, or STeam as it is known at Amazon.[51] The company was ten years old and beginning to show real promise, but Bezos was troubled at how it was running meetings.

He felt company decision forums were stale and had no real spark. There were too many PowerPoint presentations. He worried this approach stifled discussion, innovation, and how Amazon came up with new ideas. He quickly typed his thoughts into an email, and at 6:02 p.m., he pressed send.

One can only imagine how his senior leaders felt when the email arrived in their inboxes with the subject line "No powerpoint presentations from now on at STeam."

PowerPoint is the life support that many senior teams use to run their meetings, and Amazon was no different. You dump your thoughts into bullet points and go through them in painstaking detail with your colleagues.

In the email to the STeam, Bezos outlined why he was killing PowerPoint presentations and replacing them with a four-page narrative memo.[52] He thought that storytelling and carefully structured story-based arguments would solve the innovation problem at Amazon. That's how much trust he was putting in storytelling.

Bezos didn't want any old thing written down in the memo—he wanted team members to pause and consider the narrative. "Well structured, narrative text is what we're after rather than just text. If someone builds a list of bullet points in Word, that would be just as bad as powerpoint," he said.

In the email, he gave some reasons why his new structure would foster innovation and creativity. He wanted them to think more deeply about how they were presenting the story. "The reason writing a 4 page memo is harder than 'writing' a 20 page PowerPoint is because the narrative structure of a good memo forces better thought and better understanding of what's more important than what, and how things are related."

He knew standing at a laptop and broadcasting boring information wasn't working. "PowerPoint-style presentations somehow give permission to gloss over ideas, flatten out any sense of relative importance, and ignore the interconnectedness of ideas," he said.

Since that evening in 2004, the narrative memo has become central to how Amazon communicates new ideas, deciphers information, solves problems, and innovates. I think you'd agree that it hasn't fared all that badly since.

Where did Bezos get his inspiration for this change at Amazon? He had long been an admirer of how Warren Buffett communicates through his annual letter to the shareholders of Berkshire Hathaway and had used this technique over the last twenty years to tell the story of the growth of Amazon.

In his 2017 letter to shareholders, Bezos took the opportunity to praise the narrative memo approach as a central element of why Amazon is so successful at customer service.[53] He gave valuable insight into the challenge of producing a good memo. It's worth parsing his words to examine their clarity:

> What do you need to achieve high standards in a particular domain area? First, you have to be able to *recognize* what good looks like in that domain. Second, you must have realistic expectations for how hard it should be (how much work it will take) to achieve that result—the *scope*.
>
> Let me give you two examples. One is a sort of toy illustration but it makes the point clearly, and another is a real one that comes up at Amazon all the time.

Perfect Handstands

A close friend recently decided to learn to do a perfect free-standing handstand. No leaning against a wall. Not for just a few seconds. Instagram-good. She decided to start her journey by taking a handstand workshop at her yoga studio. She then practiced for a while but wasn't getting the results she wanted. So, she hired a handstand coach. Yes, I know what you're thinking, but evidently this is an actual thing that exists. In the very first lesson, the coach gave her some wonderful advice. "Most people," he said, "think that if they work hard, they should be able to master a handstand in about two weeks. The reality is that it takes about six months of daily practice. If you think you should be able to do it in two weeks, you're just going to end up quitting." Unrealistic beliefs on scope—often hidden and undiscussed—kill high standards. To achieve high standards yourself or as part of a team, you need to form and proactively communicate realistic beliefs about how hard something is going to be—something this coach understood well.

Six-Page Narratives

We don't do PowerPoint (or any other slide-oriented) presentations at Amazon. Instead, we write narratively structured six-page memos. We silently read one at the beginning of each meeting in a kind of "study hall." Not surprisingly, the quality of these memos varies widely. Some have the clarity of angels singing. They are brilliant and thoughtful and set up the meeting for high-quality discussion. Sometimes they come in at the other end of the spectrum.

In the handstand example, it's pretty straightforward to *recognize* high standards. It wouldn't be difficult to lay out in detail the requirements of a well-executed handstand, and then you're either doing it or you're not. The writing example is very different. The difference between a great memo and an average one is much squishier. It would be extremely hard to write down the detailed requirements that make up a great memo. Nevertheless, I find that much of the time readers react to great memos very similarly. They know it when they see it. The standard is there, and it is real, even if it's not easily describable.

Here's what we've figured out. Often, when a memo isn't great, it's not the writer's inability to *recognize* the high standard, but instead a wrong expectation on scope: they mistakenly believe a high-standards, six-page memo can be written in one or two days or even a few hours, when really it might take a week or more! They're trying to perfect a handstand in just two weeks, and we're not coaching them right. The great memos are written and rewritten, shared with colleagues who are asked to improve the work, set aside for a couple of days, and then edited again with a fresh mind. They simply can't be done in a day or two. The key point here is that you can improve results through the simple act of teaching scope—that a great memo probably should take a week or more.

In this extract, we can see the skill of Bezos as a storyteller in full view. In the highly technical context of an SEC filing, he shares a story to illustrate his point about the power of storytelling. He explains that the reason the narrative memo works so well is that it takes critical thinking and practice to perfect. It is the exact opposite of a bullet-point-strewn presentation, where everybody is mediocre and more focused on stealing attention rather than on shedding any real light on the topic.

In the years since the narrative approach was first proposed by Bezos, the technique has developed, and now a six-page memo is required for senior management meetings.

Amazon has adapted this narrative style in other areas of the business too. One approach it uses in many of its business units is called "working backwards." In a post on the question-and-answer site Quora, Ian McAllister, a director at Amazon, explained how it works.[54]

"We try to work backwards from the customer, rather than starting with an idea for a product and trying to bolt customers onto it. While working backwards can be applied to any specific product decision, using this approach is especially important when developing new products or features."

McAllister highlighted how the storytelling approach is adapted to imagine what a successful outcome will look like from the start of a project. "For new initiatives, a product manager typically starts by writing an internal press release announcing the finished product." One of the key challenges in this approach to storytelling is considering who the story is aimed at. "The target audience for the press release is the new/updated product's customers, which can be retail customers or internal users of a tool or technology. Internal press releases are centered around the customer problem, how current solutions (internal or external) fail, and how the new product will blow away existing solutions," said McAllister.

Why do they do it? Because if the story isn't very good, then maybe the product won't be up to much either. McAllister elaborated: "If the benefits listed don't sound very interesting or exciting to customers, then perhaps they're not (and shouldn't be built)." But rather than give up, this is useful information that should inform the process. "Instead, the product manager should keep iterating on the press release until they've come up with benefits that actually sound like benefits. Iterating on a press release is a lot less expensive than iterating on the product itself (and quicker!)."

Here is the internal press release structure McAllister suggests works best:

- **Heading**: Name the product in a way the reader (i.e., your target customers) will understand.

- **Sub-heading**: Describe who the market for the product is and what benefit they get. One sentence only, underneath the title.

- **Summary**: Give a summary of the product and the benefit. Assume the reader will not read anything else, so make this paragraph good.

- **Problem**: Describe the problem your product solves.

- **Solution**: Describe how your product elegantly solves the problem.

- **Quote from you**: Include a quote from a spokesperson in your company.

- **How to get started**: Describe how easy it is to get started.

- **Customer quote**: Provide a quote from a hypothetical customer that describes how they experienced the benefit.

- **Closing and call to action**: Wrap it up and give pointers where the reader should go next.

What did you learn from Amazon? Could you abolish PowerPoint for internal meetings? Would it mean there would be more time for better discussions where people debate and argue from informed viewpoints? What about writing a press release for every innovation? It will make any idea you want to launch much more market-ready. Give it a try.

Points to Ponder

- Who speaks publicly for your organization? Are they good enough, or could they improve? What difference would it make to have more people able to be the public face of your brand?

- What is the standard for presentations in your organization? Is it death by PowerPoint? What would it take to transform it into stories?

- How good are you at opening up and sharing stories about your process? If you are still focused on the shiny end result, then you need to change.

- The next time you have a new product idea, follow the Amazon way and write a press release about it at the very start of the process. Watch how much easier the innovation process flows.

Exercises for You

- Identify a group of between six and ten people in your organization who have the raw potential to be great communicators. Get them the resources and story training they need to represent your organization in public.

- Bring your mission to life by getting people to talk about it. Once a month, we have a guest speaker at MediaHQ. Our mission is to help our users make the news. We get people to talk about what making the news means to them.

- Ban bad PowerPoint by getting your team the training they need to communicate with stories. Make sure meetings are engagements and debates around memos, not bullet points on slides.

Public Speaking

The Next Time You Face a Crowd, Tell a Story

I can remember exactly where I was when I realized I wanted to be really good at public speaking. In January of 1999, I started working for a political party in Ireland called the Progressive Democrats. I was employed as a press officer. My job was to act as a conduit between politicians, candidates, and the media.

From the outside, the premise of the job was simple:

Get the candidates elected by connecting their stories with as many voters in their constituencies as possible.

My first big tests were the local government elections that June. My job was to help get a reasonable number of new local councillors elected and to sow the seeds for the party's future.

To prepare, we decided to hold a candidate workshop to teach the aspiring politicians how to prepare for the election. My boss—the party's general secretary—gave me a forty-five-minute slot on that day to talk about how to deal with the media. The mere thought of it induced panic—I didn't have a clue how to even start a presentation that long.

I muddled through my talk and nobody died, least of all me. The speaker immediately after me had worked in politics before embarking on a successful career in public relations. His brief was to talk about how to organize a ground campaign.

"I'm up there with chalk flying and sketching these things out and I looked into the room and everybody's head was down busily taking notes, and this shock went through me and I thought, 'Jesus, they're buying this shit.'"

Robert McKee, world-renowned story consultant

Not only did he have no slides; he had just one small page of notes he looked at occasionally. What did he do? He told stories about campaigns, successes, disasters, great wins, and nail-biting defeats. The audience laughed and they listened. It was obvious they were tuned in.

Watching him perform was when I decided I wanted to get better at public speaking. I wanted to know what it felt like to have the audience in the palm of my hand, hanging on my every word.

Years later, I interviewed world-renowned story teacher Robert McKee, who counts John Cleese, Russell Crowe, Peter Jackson, and Geoffrey Rush among his many alumni. He described the moment he realized public speaking was what he wanted to do. In graduate school, he had a lazy professor who told his class each student had to teach one lesson that semester by picking a piece of writing to analyze. McKee picked the play *Miss Julie* by August Strindberg. He recalled what happened when he stood at the front of the class to teach.

> "I'm up there with chalk flying and sketching these things out and I looked into the room and every-body's head was down busily taking notes, and this shock went through me and I thought, 'Jesus, they're buying this shit'…And the sense of power was over-whelming. You can put ideas into the world and people will take note."[55]

McKee also described the powerful feeling that came over him when he realized the story had both connected with and physically transformed his audience.

"You know because you can see the light going off in people's eyes. They are experiencing an awakening."[56]

The journey to achieve anything difficult starts with a burning urge, but realizing you want to get better at public speaking and actually getting better are completely different. One is the spark that gets you on the road to improvement. But then you have to start on that journey. You have to start practicing the thing you want to improve. You have to resource yourself. Let's discover how.

How Do You Get Better at Public Speaking?

How do you get better at anything? Ira Glass is recognized as one of the founders of podcasting. His radio show, *This American Life*, started out on the local public radio station WBEZ in Chicago. Its storytelling content is so compelling, it has become a must-listen show all over the world.

In 2009, Glass took part in a small series about storytelling and spoke about how to get better when you're starting out:

Nobody tells this to people who are beginners. I wish someone told me. All of us who do creative work, we get into it because we have good taste. But there is this gap. For the first couple years you make stuff, it's just not that good. It's trying to be good, it has potential, but it's not. But your taste, the thing that got you into the game, is still killer. And your taste is why your work disappoints you…Put yourself on a deadline so that every week you will finish one story. It's only by going through a volume of work that you will close that gap, and your work will be as good as your ambitions.[57]

Once I had my light-bulb moment about wanting to be good at speaking in public, I decided I wanted to close the gap Ira Glass describes.

Here are five things I do to get better at public speaking.

1. Tune In to Great Public Speakers and Learn

My first step was to tune in to great public speakers and learn. I was surrounded by politicians, which gave me plenty of examples, good and bad.

When I was really lucky, I got to write speeches for them and see how they performed. Mary Harney was my boss. She was leader of the Progressive Democrats party and the deputy prime minister of Ireland. She is also an impressive public speaker. Every year, the party had a national conference where she would give the keynote speech live on prime-time Saturday night television.

"It's only by going through a volume of work that you will close that gap, and your work will be as good as your ambitions."

Ira Glass, This American Life

There is a standard way to prepare for a live speech. You draft a script, hone it, and then practice at a teleprompter. But there was one problem: Mary didn't like teleprompters and refused to use them. Instead, she learned the whole thirty-minute speech by heart and delivered it live. Her only fail-safe was a series of hand signals, telling her to speed up or slow down, from her assistant Catherine in the audience. For those of us aware of what was really happening, watching it was terrifying, like a trapeze act with no safety net. But she always pulled it off.

Mary loves a good story and insisted on having them in every speech. She often responded to a first draft of a speech by looking for more stories, something more exciting and more engaging. She had a great ability to connect with an audience. She used people's names when she spoke to them and was able to tell a joke. Those things matter.

2. Have a Muse

A muse, by definition, is someone who acts as your inspiration. We should all have muses in our lives. I have many people I look to for inspiration, advice, and leadership. Some of them I know well, and others I admire from afar.

When it comes to public speaking, Seth Godin is my muse. Seth is one of the world's leading marketing gurus, and he first caught my attention when his seminal book *Purple Cow: Transform Your Business by Being Remarkable* came out in 2002. In the book, he talks about how to be, well, remarkable. And he acts on his advice to the letter. He is colorful and addresses his readers directly through his books, blog, and talks. The simplicity of his presentation, in person or in print, grabs your attention instantly.

Seth's great gift is being able to give talks about a single theme that are made up of a collection of stories. His slides are always simple—either a short phrase, one word, or an image. I've taken inspiration over the years about how I talk in public, and it has worked.

A few years back, I got an email from him saying the first one hundred people to reply could come to the launch of his book *Tribes* in New York and spend an afternoon with him. I replied, traveled from Ireland, and learned a huge amount from the experience.

3. Practice, Practice, Practice

In 2008, a short family holiday in an eco-retreat in the west of Ireland was an unusual setting for my public speaking to get an unexpected boost.

On Saturday morning, I went down to reception to ask some touristy questions of Noeleen, who owned the resort. I noticed a bright red contact card on her desk. Remarkably, it was marketing material I had created for my business, MediaHQ. It listed the email address and phone number to every national news desk.

She said a friend had given it to her because she was doing some publicity for the business and needed to talk to journalists. I innocently inquired how she found the experience of talking to journalists. I had no clue back then, but her answer would plunge me into the world of public speaking in a way I had never imagined.

She said when she spoke to journalists, she never really knew whether she was doing well or poorly. Sometimes she succeeded and didn't know why, and sometimes she failed and didn't know why.

Without even thinking, I asked, "Would a training course help?" She said it would be a huge help and that she was part of a local environmental business network called Greenbox. The following Monday morning, I got my first paid booking to speak in public. I was giving a public relations training course to the members of Greenbox in County Leitrim.

That booking was the start I needed. Since then, I have had hundreds of hours of practice speaking in public. I have given daylong courses and two-hour seminars. Every event and every audience is different, and I love the challenge of connecting with a new group.

4. Experiment with Different Formats

To get better, it's good to try new things. I love experimenting with different public speaking formats. Each new format I've mastered has given me new communications skills and a different way to connect with an audience.

A few years ago, I was invited to a media "unconference" organized by O'Reilly Media in Phoenix, Arizona. One of the ways the delegates entertained themselves at the end of each day was by performing a talk format they devised called Ignite. An Ignite Talk includes twenty slides, each shown for fifteen seconds. And here's the mad thing: the slides change automatically. It's all over in five minutes, and it's exciting and terrifying in equal measure. It's the public speaking equivalent of a roller coaster. Late one night, I submitted a talk title for the conference I thought no one would like:

Why the Irish Sport of Hurling Should Take Over the World

To my great amazement, they loved the idea, and I was asked to perform my Ignite Talk in front of two hundred of the world's most influential journalists and media executives—no pressure.

The great thing about the format is how brief it is. It naturally accentuates everything that is great about storytelling and limits the things that might make you dull or produce less impact. The short time available encourages you to make big points with images and few words. If a slide is terrible, it lasts only fifteen seconds, and if it's amazing, the same rule applies. When you're in the middle of it, it feels like a runaway train.

The hurling talk was great fun, and I'm such a convert to the Ignite format that I use it on storyteller training days to shock people out of the normal way they present. I've also used it in work to break the ice by getting colleagues to present about a topic outside of work they are passionate about. It will always reveal something about someone.

5. Go to the Edge of Your Comfort Zone

One of the ways to get better is to seek out new learning experiences. When you are at the edge of your comfort zone, it means you are really learning. One performance and storytelling experience that has helped me hugely is immersive theatre. It's a drama format in which you, as an audience member, participate in the story.

A few years ago, I went to New York on a learning trip. A friend had recommended a play called *Sleep No More*. I was intrigued. "What is it?" I inquired. He replied, "It's an immersive play based on Shakespeare's *Macbeth*, set in a large hotel in Manhattan. It's like taking the top off the television and getting in. You've never experienced anything like it before; trust me. You follow the play around the hotel for hours. Your head will be spinning."

I was instantly hooked. What a mad way to tell a story. A week later, I was standing in line outside the McKittrick Hotel in Chelsea, New York, waiting to be ushered into the one-hundred-room building for the start of the *Sleep No More* performance. There was a nervous excitement in the air. No one knew what was going to happen. I knew from talking to people in the line that some of them had been there many times before and were back for more. When I asked why, I got vague answers. One guy said, "It's hard to describe; you'll never experience anything like it." I had butterflies in my stomach and was nervous with excitement.

Upon entering the building, we split into groups and were given a ticket. When my group's number was called, we were brought in for a briefing. We were all given white eye masks to wear. The mask was to separate the audience from the performers. We were given strict instructions: no talking, and never remove your mask.

"It's an immersive play based on Shakespeare's Macbeth, set in a large hotel in Manhattan. It's like taking the top off the television and getting in."

Anyone who was in a group of friends was told to split up. Before the briefing ended, we were to remember that "fortune favors the brave." The words rang in my ears. We were then invited to go into an industrial lift by a man with a mask, and my heart began to beat really fast. The lift stopped, seemingly at random at different floors, and he chose who would leave. After five minutes, I was the only person left as we arrived at the top floor. He gestured for me to leave the lift, gave me a gentle push in the small of my back, and I was out. As I was trying to get my bearings, two actors—a man and a woman—brushed past me at speed. They were arguing; I decided to follow. They went into a room, so did I, and I stood in the corner observing their row—just me and them and my sense of excitement.

And so the mad journey went on for over an hour. I was catching small moments of stories around the hotel and trying to piece them together in my head. It was a completely immersive experience: the sounds, the music, even the smells made me and all the other audience members part of the story, not mere observers.

After what seemed like an age, I found myself watching an actor—a tall, elegant woman in her midfifties—playing Lady Macduff dancing with a much younger man. They were almost in a trance. As the dancing came to an end, the crowd began to disperse. I was about to turn away when Lady Macduff turned to me and whispered in my ear: "Stay here; I want to talk to you." I was stunned. I hadn't heard anyone talk in well over an hour.

She led me a couple of paces to a wall of black panels. She touched a panel and it opened like a door. She led me inside. At this stage, my heart was leaping out of my chest. What was happening? She raised her hands and removed my mask. I couldn't quite believe it. We were talking and the masks were off. Was this not against the rules? I now knew what they meant when they said "fortune favors the brave."

The room was small and dark. She brought me over to an armchair in the corner and sat me down. There was a light and a fan blowing a net curtain into my face. It was disorientating and nearly had me in a trance. She went to a cupboard and got me a drink, a glass of milk. She then leaned in and told me a secret about the play and told me to be on my way. It was over almost as soon as it began.

I bounced out of there excited, full of energy, and determined to solve the mystery. In the remaining hours, I attended a funeral, dug a grave, visited a mental hospital, was chased out of a pub, and was locked in a wardrobe. It was the most amazing storytelling experience I had ever experienced.

In the years since, I've been to many immersive performances, and each time I learn something new about how to perform a story. Maybe about the power of empathy and fear or challenging the conventional way of doing it. The lessons aren't always easy to translate or immediately applicable, but that's what makes them even more powerful. They have taught me the power of continually resourcing my creativity with new people, new places, and new experiences.

Points to Ponder

- How often do you practice public speaking? Are you a willing participant, or are you dragged kicking and screaming to the podium? The first step in getting better is to embrace it.

- Being a great public speaker is about one thing: connecting with your audience. Revisit the chapter in the book called "Understanding the Science behind Stories" and ask yourself which hormones you want your talk to trigger. Shape your stories to get the reactions you want. Try it; it's like magic.

- What is your public speaking style now? Assess it, and be honest with yourself. Are you overly reliant on slides with bullet points and dry technical information? How could you make it more engaging? One step is to put stories about people in your next presentation. Watch how it changes the audience reaction.

- Who do you admire as a really good public speaker? Write out a list of people and spend some time studying what they do.

Exercises for You

- Organize an Ignite event with your colleagues. To make it easier, insist that everyone pick something they love that has nothing to do with work. It is a great way to free everyone up and take the pressure off. The rules are simple:

  - Twenty slides (no title slides, no GIFs or videos)

  - Fifteen seconds each slide

  - Someone other than the presenter does the time and the slide changing.

  - It all ends at five minutes, whether the presenter is finished or not.

- The next time you have to present, commit yourself to telling at least one story.

- Find a way to practice public speaking regularly with new audiences. The more practice you get, the better you will be.

Brand Newsroom

Tell the Story on Your Own Terms

Most organizations communicate to capture people's attention. They find and nurture a captive audience and communicate with them regularly to change their behavior. They want them to purchase, donate, influence, or start or stop doing something.

For almost a century, from the 1890s, the ways you could connect your story to your audience were set in stone. You either took out a checkbook and bought advertising space or used a public relations professional to craft your story and present it to journalists in an engaging and digestible format. It was simple: you either bought the attention or earned it for a fee.

The different communications professions were organized on strictly delineated bases. When things were simple, there was just marketing, advertising, and public relations. The marketeers found the opportunities and created excitement, the advertisers created great stories, and once you had enough money, you could buy the best ideas and the most attention. PR people leaned on creativity and contacts to create great stories that had amazing impact. They controlled the access, and they shaped the outcome.

And then along came the internet, particularly social media, and everything changed. Having a smartphone gave everyone the ability to be a media outlet or a publisher of content in their own right. You no longer needed a printing press or a broadcast mast to be famous. You just needed great ideas and the ability to connect with your audiences. All of a sudden, everyone had the potential to have a slingshot like David.

When old ways are ripped up, it creates huge opportunities, but new rules of engagement can be daunting for organizations. Sometimes the multitude of new options to earn a new audience can be almost crippling.

In Part 2, we analyzed the process of how to decide on the Magic Slice of your brand or organization. Once you know what you want to talk about and why it makes your voice unique, you have to execute it. You know what you want to do, and now you have to stop thinking about it. You have to act on it.

One really good way to achieve this is through a blog or a "brand newsroom." What is a brand newsroom? Simply:

A place where you publish journalism-standard stories about your brand on your own website.

It's communicating to a high standard on your own terms by cutting out the intermediary and going straight to the audience.

In communications terms, blogging has traveled a long distance from being a fringe activity and the preserve of obscure hobbyists to being a crucial mainstream tool used by the most dynamic brands in the world, including Virgin, Microsoft, and Apple.

I want to examine some great examples to discover:

1. What a brand newsroom looks like

2. How it works in practice

3. How you can use it as a tool to tell great stories from your Magic Slice

In this chapter, we're going to look at three examples of brand newsrooms. They are:

1. **Marriott Hotels**: a global brand that used brand newsrooms to light a spark

2. **Hackney Council**: creators of a local newspaper in London that was so successful it caused a crisis

3. **Intercom**: the Irish customer communications software that is redefining the standard for great brand communications

"Why the heck would anyone want to read a blog from me?"

Seventy-six-year-old Bill Marriott in 2006

Marriott Hotels—
Powerful Brand Storytelling

The first example I want to share with you is Marriott, a long-established hotel brand that decided to use a brand newsroom to make an impact on its audience by telling stories from its Magic Slice. It all happened when it hired a new head of communications.

In December 2006, Kathleen Matthews started as executive vice president of communications and public affairs for the Marriott.[58] Matthews has storytelling in her veins after spending the previous twenty-five years working as a news anchor for an ABC news affiliate in Washington, DC.

In her new role, she had a simple idea to use stories to transform how the Marriott brand communicated. She had a hunch that telling stories through a charismatic leader would work for the hotel brand.

She wanted to start a blog with Bill Marriott, who was the second generation of the family in the business that was founded by his father. At that stage, Bill was seventy-six years old and wondered whether anyone would be curious about what he had to say: "Why the heck would anyone want to read a blog from me?" he asked. Marriott was old school and didn't use a computer, so he struck a deal with Kathleen Matthews—he would dictate a blog post once a week, and she would get the story out to their customers.

Bill Marriott's weekly updates give real insight and perspective into running a global business. His longevity is an asset and allows him a unique perspective spanning three generations. His Magic Slice is about food, family, running a business, history, and politics. He has the benefit of perspective and experience. This quote from his first blog shows how it was a refreshingly direct approach:

> "Bottom line, I believe in communicating with the customer, and the internet gives me a whole new way of doing that on a global scale. I'd rather engage directly in dialogue with you because that's how we learn and grow as a company. So tell me what you think."[59]

The blog was the successful beginning of the Marriott storytelling journey: a small brand newsroom focused on its leader, sharing one blog post a week. Since then, it has grown into almost a media conglomerate. In three years, Matthews transformed how Marriott communicated. She used her nose for a story to power how it connected with its customers.

As Bill's blog gained traction, the group decided to invest in storytelling by hiring top talent. In 2013, Marriott hired Karin Timpone, from the Walt Disney Corporation, and a year later added her former Disney colleague, David Beebe. They immediately began to make a major impact on Marriott's storytelling. In 2014, Marriott set up its own content studio and started producing short films.

In 2015, Marriott created a successful TV show called *The Navigator Live*; an Emmy award-winning short film, *Two Bellmen*; and a personalized online travel magazine, *Marriott Bonvoy Traveler*.

These initiatives worked and resulted in impressive numbers that included:

- High customer engagement and a deeper relationship with customers

- Millions of dollars in direct sales revenue

- Content licensing deals with other media outlets. That's how good the stories were.

With the successes, it has continued to grow the storytelling team, adding talent from media companies like CBS and Variety. During this time, it also built a culture of storytelling driven from within the company.

Marriott delivers authentic stories it is happy to let speak for themselves rather than wallpapering them with branding. It has also partnered with many social media content creators to leverage the brand to new audiences.

Reflect on the audience step of the Magic Slice process. The first lesson is that Marriott's approach worked because of Kathleen Matthews's instinct for knowing and connecting with its audiences.

The second lesson is how Matthews changed the way Marriott communicated. It is:

"To enact real cultural change in how an organization communicates, you need to dedicate yourself to one small idea that could have a big impact."

Once Bill Marriott's blog succeeded, everyone could see the potential.

In Part 2, I outlined how powerful it is to find your Magic Slice. It is a place of true and meaningful connection with your customers, and once you get there, you will want to make sure you stay. The next case study proves that some organizations will go to great lengths to keep their Magic Slice—even repeatedly break the law.

Hackney Council—Breaking the Law to Tell Your Story

A brand newsroom doesn't always have to be a website. When the London Borough of Hackney (Hackney Council) decided to publish its own newspaper, *Hackney Today*, in 2002, it caused total consternation among the competing local newspapers and set off a chain reaction that would, somewhat incongruously, see its storytelling machine banned by the UK government.

Hackney Today newspaper was an idea born out of the council's frustration with the cost of the traditional way of sharing stories, which meant it had to pay high advertising fees to local newspapers for statutory notice advertisements.[60]

A statutory notice is an official communication informing residents about planning, traffic, and other matters that might affect them, which the council is legally obliged to disclose in a newspaper that is published more than once a month.

The council thought there was a better way and decided to beat the local newspapers at their own game by creating a free fortnightly paper. It was an ambitious project that would allow the council to connect stories from its Magic Slice directly with citizens. The Magic Slice topics are:

- Local news

- Events

- Services

- Education

- Housing

- Community

Hackney Today was so successful at sharing the council's stories that it reached all one hundred thousand homes in the borough and redefined the local media landscape. It was well designed, colorful, and full of great local-interest stories and good photography.

The area is also served by two traditional, privately owned newspapers—the *Hackney Gazette* and the *Hackney Citizen*—which found it hard to compete with the quality of the council's newspaper. In the face of such stiff competition, the *Hackney Gazette* could only manage a weekly circulation of just over 1,300 copies with a cover price of

£1 ($1.39). Its circulation has fallen steadily since its peak of 13,389 copies in 2002.

Hackney Council's efforts at connecting with the local community were so successful, it completely distorted the local media market and upset the commercial newspapers. Hackney's citizens preferred the council's free newspaper over the paid-for commercial alternatives, and those papers weren't taking it lightly.

Rival *Gazette* editor Ramzy Alwakeel wasn't happy to be competing with the council's Magic Slice for attention:

> "I believe the existence of a fortnightly council freesheet in 2019 is a significant obstruction to genuine local newspapers—not just by taking away advertising but perhaps more significantly by fooling time-pressed readers into thinking they've already had their local news and therefore don't need to pick up the Gazette or the Citizen."[61]

Hackney Council's story disruption was so successful that, in 2011, the UK government stepped in to stop *Hackney Today* and other newspapers run by local councils.

Why? It ruled that councils must not publish newspapers more than four times a year because they were breaking the Publicity Code—a set of regulations approved by the parliament to try to stop taxpayer money from being spent on newspapers. Undeterred by the law of the land, Hackney Council continued to publish its paper.

This intransigence in the face of the law forced the government's hand. It went one step further by strengthening the code with the Local Audit and Accountability Act 2014. At the time, the government minister in charge, Communities Secretary Sajid Javid, said:

> "An independent free press is vital for local democracy and it's important that we support them in holding local leaders to account. Councils shouldn't undermine local democracy by publishing their own newspapers more often than quarterly."[62]

His claims of *Hackney Today*'s undermining of democracy fell on deaf ears, and the council continued to defy the government by claiming *Hackney Today* was the "most cost-effective way of getting information out to residents and reached the most people."

In April 2018, new powers were brought in for the secretary of state for communities and local government, and the council was ordered to cease publication of *Hackney Today*. But it decided to fight the directive. The council lost a judicial review in May 2019 and requested the right to appeal, but this was rejected by judges that August. It had lost the right to tell its story its way.

On receiving the judgment, a council spokesperson conceded defeat by saying, "There are no more legal options available to the council, so *Hackney Today* will no longer be published fortnightly." The spokesperson then sounded a positive note. "The council is now considering how it can best continue to keep the borough's diverse communities informed of services and opportunities available to them in a cost-effective way which complies with the government's legal direction."

Hackney Today had been in print for seventeen years. It published its last fortnightly issue on June 24, 2019.

It cost the council more than £500,000 ($700,000) to produce, but the freesheet actually saved the council money, as it didn't have to spend tens of thousands of pounds on statutory notices in the local press. It is now available online and complies with the law by publishing four times a year.

Since then, the council's dedication to storytelling hasn't waned. It has invested its resources in an impressive online brand newsroom and a new print publication, *Hackney Life*, which focuses on local events, along with *Hackney News*, a weekly email newsletter.

I love this story because it shows how a dedicated and committed storyteller will face down any obstacle to connect with their audience. The communications team in Hackney Council decided to create a free local newspaper as its story platform, not because it was easy, but because it was the best way to communicate stories from its Magic Slice. It stayed committed to the project even when its storytelling was judged illegal. That's impressive. It's also impressive how it adapted to the law by publishing online and maintaining a strong bond with the community.

To finish this chapter, I want to take a deeper look into customer communications software company Intercom, which produces the platinum standard when it comes to communicating directly with your customers through your brand newsroom. From the start, Intercom has embraced storytelling as a central element of its marketing and communications strategy. It has invested heavily in talent, technology, and know-how and is a great example of what's possible when you are committed to the craft of storytelling. Let's take a detailed look behind how it does it so well.

Intercom—Using Stories to Connect Customers

Intercom was started in 2011 by four Irish engineers, Eoghan McCabe, Des Traynor, Ciaran Lee, and David Barrett. The founders started off with a simple goal: to build great software that people loved.

Intercom makes tools that enable its clients to communicate directly with their customers. They do this through the customers' own websites, through Intercom's web and mobile apps, and through email. You've probably used an Intercom product without knowing it. You know that blue chat button that pops up in the corner of home pages? That's Intercom's flagship feature.

Quite quickly, it was obvious it was onto something. During its first three major funding rounds, Intercom grew like Japanese knotweed, from $1 million in annual recurring revenue to $50 million. During this initial growth, Intercom had more than 400 million conversations on its platform and built a portfolio of seventeen thousand paying clients.

One of its key growth tools was storytelling. Intercom's starting point was building tools for businesses to connect directly with customers, so blogging was a perfect fit. In addition to his job as innovation lead at the company, Des Traynor took to blogging with gusto and was responsible for ninety-three of their first one hundred posts.

Over that time, Intercom's storytelling skills developed from a loose collection of posts giving advice to startups to something much more strategic. Traynor quickly settled on the Intercom Magic Slice:

Stories about how to best connect with your customers.

As the company grew, it embraced a storytelling approach. In 2014, it hired John Collins to lead its content team. Up to that point, he had been working at the *Irish Times* as a journalist and editor.

At this stage, Intercom was seriously funded. But instead of spending all the money on advertising and traditional PR, it doubled down on a storytelling strategy. It hired a team of professional journalists and content creators in-house to do what the software does: talk directly to customers.

Collins quickly made his mark on how Intercom was telling stories.[63] He began by focusing on its Magic Slice and how it was telling stories. Collins knew its customers didn't want to hear from him or the other content creators on the team; they wanted to hear from the experts working at Intercom. Its Magic Slice became just that:

Expert stories on how to better connect your business with your customers.

It went one step further. It decided it wasn't going to compete with the news agenda or what was topical on the internet on any given day. Why? Because you pour a whole load of effort into news-focused content, and then it's out of date before it has enough time to be relevant. Instead, it focused all of its content on evergreen, universal themes. One look on the blog will show you what this looks like in practice. Headlines include:

"The Art of the Customer Follow-Up and Delightful Customer Service"

"Built for You: How Customer Feedback Informs What We Ship"

"Key Strategies to Successfully Scale Your Customer Support Team"

Collins says that evergreen content works because it doesn't date (they've even removed the date of some posts), and it's not trying to drive clicks. If the content you create is free from the need to get attention at all costs, then it can be something else, something more substantial that is likely to attract customers who will stay around. It's a good lesson.

Collins has also worked hard to get story contributors from every department in the company. He says company blogs often fail because they rely too heavily on one employee, and that one employee is often the CEO, writing content on the weekend. It's a strategy doomed to fail. He says that you should use every strategy possible to avoid this overreliance and that using "ghostwriters" or interviewing in-house experts are two good ways around the problem.

Collins believes in competition and incentives, and he shares the internet content stats with the employees. This highlights who has written the most popular post in a given week. He says it's always great for discussion and engagement and believes that a little bit of in-house competition is healthy.

Another key element of Intercom's content strategy is using its significant financial heft to publish books. It has produced a wide range of books on varying aspects of its mission to help users connect with their customers.

And let's be clear: these are not e-books. It is an important distinction; it is keen to stress. When Intercom had the first title in planning, CEO Eoghan McCabe asked them to stop referring to them as e-books, as he felt it devalued what the company was doing. It wasn't selling—it was educating, informing, and helping its users. The theme of the books is "Intercom on…" and they include titles like:

Intercom on Sales

Intercom on Onboarding

Intercom on Marketing

Intercom on Starting Up

Intercom on Customer Support

Intercom on Jobs-to-Be-Done

It is easy to see a correlation with the blog and a focus on evergreen themes that will attract potential customers who are curious and want to learn and grow.

Intercom has never slavishly followed content marketing trends that fetishized clicks at all costs, practices that sometimes seem more focused on capitalizing on the world's fractured attention than on giving it something that will cure it. Instead of this snap-happy approach, Intercom is motivated to build a relationship with potential users by sharing knowledge and expertise.

In 2017, Collins took a stand against what he saw as the base tendencies of content marketing and shared a post on the Intercom blog entitled "Why We're Dropping the Term 'Content Marketing.'" His post pulled no punches, and he took aim at what he thought was wrong with the new wave of content marketing.

> "Innovative companies rushed to create their own internal newsrooms staffed by journalists, only then to have them crank out product announcements and press releases. It's little wonder many view content marketing as a series of hacks taken straight from a mythical playbook called "0 to 10,000 customers in 5 easy steps."[64]

Collins believed there were two distinct types of organizations embracing content. In the first group, he said, there are companies that are really successful with content marketing driven by aggressive email captures, funnels, and A/B tests, which he called playbook content marketing. In the second group, there are companies (including Intercom) that believe if you focus on publishing great content, you won't actually need to do much marketing to attract people to your product. He also name-checked Basecamp, Figma, and Algolia in this group.

Collins says the first job of content creators is to produce something people will want to read, watch, or listen to. It decided to change the job titles of those creating the stories for Intercom. So out went titles like content marketing manager, and in came editor, producer, and researcher.

Interestingly, he said that if Intercom were driven by marketing considerations rather than editorial ones,[65] it would never do things like publish a 120-page hardcover book[66] and then sell it at a loss. Paradoxically, he believes that by focusing on the quality of the publication rather than on marketing hacks to get readers to download something of poorer quality, it attracts more than enough potential customers to make the whole exercise worthwhile. That's definitely an easier decision to make when you've got millions in funding, but it's an interesting perspective.

Collins never shies away from giving an opinion—he believes it's essential in his line of work. What he doesn't think is necessary is being contentious or difficult. He thinks the two often get confused. He believes the last thing the world needs is more mediocre material. He cites the example of newsjacking (when a brand or firm mentions or creates a campaign centered around a major, well-discussed news item). This worked well when it was new and innovative but now falls flat on its face or comes across as tone-deaf.

At the end of his clarion-call post for the end to content marketing, Collins outlined three steps he would love every storyteller to use to put the reader first:

- Create an editorial calendar of what you're going to publish.

- Start brainstorming ideas from all around the company.

- Don't be afraid to have an opinion.

Intercom's storytelling tools:

- **Blog**: Keep it fresh and evergreen. People want to hear from the experts. Measure, measure, and measure again.

- **Podcasts**: Be consistent in timing and the quality of content. Have the same show length and do it once a week.

- **Events**: Make sure your events tune in to your mission.

- **Books**: They're a big investment of time and budget, but they could have a longer and bigger payoff.

Intercom's storytelling lessons:

- **Know your mission and your Magic Slice**. Everything Intercom does is to help its users connect with their customers. There is a ruthless simplicity in how it executes it.

- **Decide on your style**. Have a house style, and don't keep bouncing around. You need to be consistent to build your audiences.

- **Be consistent**. Don't bite off more than you can chew. Decide what you're going to do and stick to it.

- **Resource your storytelling**. You might not have a big budget, but telling the story has to start by being someone's job. To start, make sure you give one person the time and resources to do it. You can grow it from there.

Points to Ponder

- Your brand newsroom should be the repository and engine for how you tell stories. It should be the driver of all your new ideas and be buzzing with creative energy.

- Make sure your Magic Slice Topics are visible and easily identifiable in your brand newsroom.

- When you publish stories on social media or send a press release, be sure to link back to your site.

- The recipe is simple: great headlines + human interest stories + good writing = success.

Exercises for You

- Examine how you publish news on your website now. Ask yourself, Is it fit for purpose? Does it need a redesign?

- Find three brands that have great brand newsrooms and study them closely. Here are some great questions to help you:

    o What does their main page look like? What stands out in the design?

- What does an individual post look like?

- How are they doing the photography? Images are very important.

- Organize a three-month plan to write stories that fit your Magic Slice for your brand newsroom. Here are some pointers:

  - Follow the idea process in Part 2.

  - Write good headlines.

  - Put people at the heart of the stories.

  - Remember the science, and focus on the hormones you want to trigger.

Glossary of Storytelling Tools

Before we finish, I want to give you a non-exhaustive list of tools you can use to improve your storytelling skills.

Advertising

A persuasive or informative message aimed at educating or persuading an audience. It can be delivered through a wide range of media, including:

- Audio: radio and podcasts

- Experiential: through physical objects and installations

- Online

- Print: magazines and newspapers

- Video: online, TV, and film

Animation

A short, scripted, cartoon-type film usually between sixty and ninety seconds, used to explain an organization or a product. Used frequently for service and software products due to their intangible nature. A great way to explain a story in a pithy and easy-to-remember way.

Blog Post

A story on your site about your work. Blog posts can come in many different formats:

- Announcement

- Explainer: showing how something works

- Interview

- News story

- Opinion

- Product review

Book

A document in hardback, paperback, or online format that is between thirty thousand and sixty thousand words. It can be fiction or nonfiction.

Brand Newsroom

A collection of blog posts written about your Magic Slice Topics that appears on your website. It should look like an online newsroom designed to showcase your brand. It often mixes great pictures with text stories, podcasts, and videos.

Brochure/Newspaper/Magazine

A piece of physical print that tells a collection of stories about a brand or organization.

Campaign

Stories delivered through a mixture of some of the outlined tools in this glossary, centered around a single theme to influence the behavior of a specific audience type.

Conference or Event

A collection of different speakers about the same theme. It can be part of a day, a single day, or a multiday event. It can be delivered through keynote presentations, discussions, workshops, or networking. It can be delivered in person or virtually. There are also storytelling opportunities through in-person conferences when there is an exhibition floor with many different organizations exhibiting.

Graphic Illustration or Cartoon

This is either a single drawing or a series of drawings in a particular style that tells a story. They are usually colorful and warm. They specialize in simplifying difficult concepts or stories.

Large Physical Object

This could be a place, building, or monument. It is any large physical thing that could be a vehicle. The nature of the story could be focused on:

- How it was built

- How it was formed

- The people who created it

- Its place in history, business, innovation, geography

Media Interview

This can be online, in print, or on radio or TV. It is an interview between a journalist and someone representing your organization. There are many types:

- Live interview: online, TV, or radio

- Panel discussion (more than one person)

- For comment in a news story

- For a newspaper feature

My Story Page on Your Website

Here is where you get to completely own your story. You tell it on your terms, unfiltered. Be creative and take inspiration from great examples. How can you inject some nice imagery and design into it? It should:

- Be inspirational in tone, starting with a founding story and clearly communicating your mission

- Communicate your values by its tone

- Clearly outline your organization's position and show the benefits you deliver

Packaging

The outer layer in which a product is delivered to the customer. It can include imagery, photography, or graphics. Stories are often told through competitions and brand icons or mascots.

Pitch Email

This is a single email to a journalist or a series of single emails to a number of journalists. As the name suggests, you are pitching a story, or selling it. It must be persuasive and tuned in to what the particular journalist or media outlet would usually cover. If it looks like something they have already covered, then you've got a chance. Always do the research. Know what the journalist likes and you're more likely to be pushing an open door.

Podcast

Audio-based information that allows you to tell stories in a number of different formats:

- Advice

- Interviews

- Group discussion

- Monologues: narration, opinions, or stories

- Narrative-led stories with sound inserts

- Reviews of products, services, events, or places

- Scripted drama

Presentation

A set-piece message delivered by one person to a crowd. It can be done by way of a script, with a teleprompter, or with a slide deck as visual aids. It can vary in length from a few minutes to over an hour.

Press Release or Media Release

This is a tool as old as the hills. It is the standard way journalists and newsrooms receive stories from organizations. It can be formulaic, but there is space in the headline and the quotes to tell a story. The recipe for a great headline is:

Raw idea + News hook = Great headline

If you get the headline right, then it will be a success. Obsess about it. It is what will get the world to take notice of your story.

Small Physical Object

This could be a book, pamphlet, trophy, memento, or keepsake. It is any physical object given to people to convey meaning or a message. There is a storytelling opportunity around:

- The meaning the object conveys

- The history of the object

- How the object was made

Social Media Post

Text, an image, or a piece of audio posted on a social media network. Different networks are based around different content types. The rules for success are based on strong still or video images, being succinct, and being able to capture the mood of an audience.

Still Image

This is a photograph of a person or people, a place, or a thing. Still images are either formatted as portrait, landscape, or square and come in many different styles.

Video or Film

This is a film in a digital format that can be easily shared online. It can be anywhere from ten seconds to hours long. It can come in many different formats:

- Explainer

- Interview

- Review of a product or service

Conclusion

When I was a small boy, my dad told me the story about my great-grandfather John leaving Ireland penniless in the 1880s, on a ship bound for New York. His mission: to save our family. Not only did he survive; he thrived and created a business that has lasted for generations.

My dad's tale about this mad adventure lit a spark that has endlessly fueled my fascination with the craft of telling stories.

I've been privileged to spend all of my career helping individuals, brands, and organizations hone their stories. At the start, I found it exciting but daunting. Being in charge of somebody's story is a big responsibility. On the good days, it went very well, and I had my hands on all the control levers. But on the bad days, it seemed hopeless, and I was influencing little.

As time moved on, my skills improved and I realized that not only was storytelling a great way to communicate the mission of an organization; it was the best way to achieve it.

The good news is that by reading this book, you have completed the journey in a much shorter time than I ever did. You now have a clear six-step process to find your Magic Slice, as well as a deeper understanding about what makes storytelling the most powerful way to communicate. Before I go, I want to leave you with some important points to ponder.

Start at the Beginning

Fix your mission and get everybody behind it. A clear and ambitious mission statement will act as a rallying call and eliminate confusion. If everyone knows what you are trying to achieve, then it will be easier.

Lay a Strong Foundation

Make sure you have a great foundation story told in a consistent and visually engaging way across all of your digital and physical assets. You will only be treated like a storytelling organization if you act like one.

Build a Storytelling Culture

Value storytelling at the most senior level in your organization, and resource and support it through training, practice, and policies. Take action to ensure that meetings and presentations use stories and memos instead of PowerPoints and that you run team-building and company events with a story ethos.

Tune In to Your Audiences

Tune in to your audiences all the time. The more you know about them, the more successful you will be. Tastes and behaviors change, so this work is never done. Like a good chef who tastes as they cook, you need to constantly tune in. You should have a clear sense of the "persona" of your ideal customer, and you should have a number of different primary and secondary data sources to show how they are engaging with you and your industry.

Practice Storytelling All the Time

Practice makes perfect. The biggest failing I've seen in my career is that people don't communicate enough. The only way you will improve your storytelling is by trying out a number of different things, seeing what works, applying what you learn, and starting all over again.

***

Why Did I Write This Book?

I wrote this book because I keep getting the same types of questions from individuals and organizations who want to figure out storytelling. They go like this:

"I need a storytelling strategy; where do I start?"

or

"I want to be a better storyteller but am not sure how to go about it."

or

"How can I put stories at the center of everything I communicate?"

or

"Why should I invest time and resources in developing my organization's storytelling capabilities? What are the business benefits, and who is doing it well?"

This book is my honest attempt to answer these questions. Having read it, you will no doubt appreciate there is a large research base, growing scientific evidence, and great success stories underpinning the simple idea of telling a story. Use this information and my six-step Magic Slice process to transform how you communicate.

How Do You Know If You Have Improved as a Storyteller?

Having read the content and completed the exercises, you may have a question:

"How will I know if I and my organization have become better storytellers?"

At the start of this journey, you spelled out your mission. It's the reason you exist and the most important thing you want to achieve. You will know if your storytelling is working if it is helping you achieve your mission. In a few months, revisit this section and answer these questions. They will act as a barometer to measure the progress you've made with your storytelling.

• How personally confident do you feel in storytelling?

- How often do you communicate using bullet-point slides?

- How many examples of great storytelling can you find in your organization from the last three months?

- How many new storytelling initiatives have you taken in the last three months?

- How many people in your organization currently have the skills and confidence to be interviewed by a journalist?

I thought you might find it helpful if I shared some of the "metrics" and behaviors I use to quantify my journey to become a better storyteller.

- Once a month, I prepare at least one story to tell in front of an audience. It can be any audience (internal or external), but the key is that I must prepare and measure their reaction.

- I talk to public relations and marketing students four times a year. I share my career story and make new connections. It reconnects me to my story and shares it with a new audience.

- I write for a minimum of five hours a week and hold myself accountable by keeping a spreadsheet of what I do and how I feel about it.

- Every Tuesday, I spend time researching for new stories to tell. I do this through reading books, periodicals, blogs, and social media and listening to podcasts and the radio.

- I have a weekly meeting with the MediaHQ marketing team about how our stories are resonating with our customers and how we can improve.

- Three times a year at MediaHQ, we take a fresh look at our Magic Slice and customer profile.

- I seek out new story experiences, opportunities, and people to talk to so I can educate myself.

***

In 2019, I received an email from the organizer of Bosnia and Herzegovina's largest media and marketing conference, called Play Media. She wanted me to give the opening keynote on storytelling. I instantly accepted and was excited by the challenge.

Three months later, I traveled to the city of Banja Luka, a historic place that knew all about hurt and turmoil. In the early 1990s, it was the scene of some of the worst atrocities in a devastating civil war that saw unspeakable bloodshed and devastation.

I stood on the stage in front of three hundred attendees to deliver a keynote in what was their second language. I fixed my microphone, took a sip of water, and started to talk.

Today I want to tell you about how to unlock the power of storytelling to transform how you communicate and help you achieve your mission.

My journey as a storyteller started when my father told me the story of how my great-grandfather saved our family...

You could hear a pin drop.

For the next forty minutes, the conference delegates and I went on a story roller coaster together. There were laughs and tears, and, like Robert McKee said, I could see the light coming on in their eyes. They were learning how to become storytellers, and they were enjoying it.

The cultural differences and the two-and-a-half-thousand kilometers from Dublin to Banja Luka vanished. I paused and looked out into the audience. I remembered that day twenty years earlier when I decided I wanted to get better, and I felt I'd reached an important point on the journey.

I hope this book gives you the tools, strategy, and confidence to put stories at the heart of how you and your organization communicate. Thanks for reading. I wish you every success. Happy storytelling.

About the Author

Jack Murray is an entrepreneur, story consultant, speaker, and author. He is the CEO and founder of MediaHQ, a media contacts database and press release distribution tool, and of the storytelling agency All Good Tales.

At MediaHQ, he leads a team that builds a technology platform that helps the world's top PR and communications teams connect their stories with their audiences. At All Good Tales, he helps companies define their storytelling strategies, train staff in storytelling, and share stories with their audiences.

He is a recognized expert in business storytelling and storytelling strategy. Over a twenty-five-year career, he has worked on story strategy with hundreds of brands, organizations, and communications teams. He previously worked in marketing, journalism, public relations, and politics.

Jack advises leadership, communications, and marketing teams through:

- Story training courses

- Story strategy workshops

- Keynote talks

He lives in Dublin with his wife, Alison, daughters, Matilda and Gwen, and a dog called Maxi Lopez.

You can reach him at Murraystory.com.

Acknowledgments

The seeds of this book have been germinating for years. Over the last ten years, I tried to write it many times, but it went nowhere. I realize now it was because I wasn't ready for what it takes to write a book.

I sat down many times with good intentions and ran out of steam in a few days. In truth, I didn't know what I was doing or how to get there. Then the pandemic struck and everything changed. When the world went into lockdown in March 2020, I opened a file on my computer and called it "the story book final attempt."

Fueled by the "nothing else to do" spirit of the lockdown, I started writing regularly and made steady progress. For the first time, I started talking to others about what I wanted to achieve, and I got the help, support, and encouragement I had never sought before. Without this help, this book would have not been possible.

To my wife, Alison, thank you for your love, support, and the time you afforded me to write. It wouldn't have been possible without this.

Thanks to my daughters, Matilda and Gwen, for keeping me grounded and happy and reminding me every day what's really important.

To my mam, Noreen, and my siblings, Kevin and Geraldine. Growing up next to our shop in a small town seemed to be the best place ever to learn how to tell a story. Thanks for your love and support.

Thanks to my friend John Meagher for offering great advice on the concept of the book and driving me on with really useful advice on the content.

Thank you to Celine O'Connor and Gareth Wynne for doing an amazing job of proofreading a number of different drafts of this book and giving excellent and detailed feedback that was very useful.

Thanks to my old friend Mícheál Lovett for also proofing the book and giving me invaluable feedback and encouragement at an important time.

To Ciara Losty, thanks for your gifts as a motivator. There were many days when getting to the finish line seemed impossible, and you always said the right thing to keep me tuned in.

To Stephen O'Reilly, thank you for helping me understand my own story. Without this help and the clarity it brought, I wouldn't have been able to write this book.

To Mariane Lee, you've been a great support on many projects over the years. It was great to have your design flair at the heart of this book.

To Joe Culley, thanks for coming along at an important time in this project and helping me finish strong.

To Kenneth O'Halloran, thanks for always encouraging me to write a book. Your words of support really drove me on.

Thank you to the dedicated team of people who work with me at MediaHQ and All Good Tales. Your skills, hard work, and determination help me every day and are always appreciated.

In 2008, I started my apprenticeship as a trainer and public speaker when Noeleen Tyrell booked me on a whim for my first event. Thank you, Noeleen. If it wasn't for you, this book might not exist. Since that first event, I have met thousands of people all over the world, and every one of them has helped me shape the ideas in this book. There is nothing as powerful as having your ideas validated in front of an audience.

Finally, to Maxi Lopez, thanks for being the best dog anyone could ask for.

Notes

Part 1: How to Unlcok the Power of Storytelling

1 Guy Raz and Nils Parker, *How I Built This: The Unexpected Paths to Success from the World's Most Inspiring Entrepreneurs* (London: MacMillan, 2020).

2 John Hegarty, *Hegarty on Creativity: There Are No Rules* (London: Thames and Hudson, 2014).

3 John Cleese, "John Cleese on Creativity in Management," filmed January 23, 1991, at the Grosvenor House Hotel, London, England, video, 36:59, https://www.youtube.com/watch?v=Pb5oIIPO62g.

4 Cleese, "John Cleese on Creativity in Management."

5 Cleese, "John Cleese on Creativity in Management."

6 Sugata Mitra, "Build a School in the Cloud," filmed February 2013 at TED2013, Long Beach, CA, video,

22:15, https://www.ted.com/talks/sugata_mitra_build _a_school_in_the_cloud?language=en#t-11846.

7 Mitra, "Build a School in the Cloud."

8 Mitra, "Build a School in the Cloud."

9 Mitra, "Build a School in the Cloud."

10 Mihaly Csikszentmihalyi, *Flow: The Psychology of Optimal Experience* (New York: Harper & Row, 1990).

11 Greg J. Stephens, Lauren J. Silbert, and Uri Hasson, "Speaker–Listener Neural Coupling Underlies Successful Communication," *PNAS* 107, no. 32 (2010): 14425–14430, https://doi.org/10.1073/pnas.1008662107.

12 Ushma Patel, "Hasson Brings Real Life into the Lab to Examine Cognitive Processing," Princeton University, December 5, 2011, https://www.princeton. edu/news/2011/12/05/hasson-brings-real-life -lab-examine-cognitive-processing.

13 Greg J. Stephens, Lauren J. Silbert, and Uri Hasson, "Speaker-Listener Neural Coupling Underlies Successful Communication."

14 Kim Ann Zimmermann, "Endocrine System: Facts, Functions and Diseases," Live Science, February 15, 2018, https://www.livescience.com/26496-endocrine- system.html.

15 David J. P. Phillips, "The Magical Science of Storytelling," filmed March 2017 at TEDxStockholm, Stockholm,

Sweden, video, 16:44, https://www.youtube.com/watch?v=Nj-hdQMa3uA.

16 Ferris Jabr, "How the Brain Gets Addicted to Gambling," *Scientific American*, November 1, 2013, https://www.scientificamerican.com/article/how-the-brain-gets-addicted-to-gambling/.

17 R. I. M. Dunbar, Jacques Launay, and Oliver Curry, "The Complexity of Jokes Is Limited by Cognitive Constraints on Mentalizing," *Human Nature* 27 (2016): 130–140, https://link.springer.com/article/10.1007/s12110-015-9251-6#citeas.

18 Holly Blake, "How Your Body Reacts to Stress," *Smithsonian Magazine*, August 9, 2017, https://www.smithsonianmag.com/science-nature/what-happens-your-body-when-youre-stressed-180964357/.

19 Karen Kangas Dwyer and Marlina M. Davidson, "Is Public Speaking Really More Feared than Death?" *Communication Research Reports* 29, no. 2 (2012): 99–107, https://www.researchgate.net/publication/271993200_Is_Public_Speaking_Really_More_Feared_Than_Death.

Part 2: The Six-Step Magic Slice Process

20 "Vision and Business Idea," IKEA, accessed June 3, 2021, https://www.ikea.com/ie/en/this-is-ikea/about-us-vision-and-business-idea-pub9cd02291.

21 "Partnering to Support Children's Rights and

Development—LEGO Group, LEGO Foundation and UNICEF," LEGO, March 12, 2015, https://www.lego.com/en-dk/aboutus/news/2019/november/childrens-rights-and-development/.

22 David Tweed, "Brick by Brick: Inside Lego," November 1, 2017, Bloomberg Markets and Finance, video, 21:30, https://www.youtube.com/watch?v=SnI56MU6H_0.

23 "History," Warby Parker, accessed June 5, 2021, https://www.warbyparker.com/history.

24 "About Sony," Sony Canada Corporate Website, accessed May 29, 2021, http://corporate.sony.ca/html/sonyinfo/index.html.

25 Ovidijus Jurevicius, "McDonald's Mission Statement," Strategic Management Insight, September 14, 2013, https://strategicmanagementinsight.com/mission-statements/mcdonalds-mission-statement.html.

26 "Core Values," Patagonia, accessed June 3, 2021, https://eu.patagonia.com/ie/en/core-values/.

27 "Bendtner in Trouble over 'Paddy' Pants," *Irish Times*, June 15, 2012, https://www.irishtimes.com/sport/soccer/bendtner-in-trouble-over-paddy-pants-1.1076278.

28 Mark Sweney, "Paddy Power's Oscar Pistorius Ad to Be Pulled after Record 5,200 Complaints," *Guardian*, March 5, 2014, https://www.theguardian.com/media/2014/mar/05/paddy-power-oscar-pistorius-ad-withdrawn-immediate-effect.

29 Dan Griffin, "Paddy Power to Be Censured for 'Immigrants Jump In' Ad," *Irish Times*, October 7, 2015, https://www.irishtimes.com/business/media-and-marketing/paddy-power-tobe-censured-for-immigrants-jump-in-ad-1.2382283.

30 Live Science Staff, "Study Suggests Why Gut Instincts Work," Live Science, February 8, 2009, https://www.livescience.com/3289-study-suggests-gut-instincts-work.html.

31 Joel L. Voss and Ken A. Paller, "An Electrophysiological Signature of Unconscious Recognition Memory," *Nature Neuroscience* 12 (2009): 349–355, https://www.nature.com/articles/nn.2260.

32 Albert Bigelow Paine, *Mark Twain: A Biography*, vol. 2, 1886–1910 (Jazzybee Verlag, 2018), 208.

33 Inc. Staff, "How Spanx Got Started," *Inc.*, January 20, 2012, https://www.inc.com/sara-blakely/how-sara-blakley-started-spanx.html.

34 Inc. Staff, "How Spanx Got Started."

35 Inc. Staff, "How Spanx Got Started."

36 Young Lee, "David Hieatt, Founder of Hiut Denim—Exclusive Interview," Heddels, May 9, 2013, https://www.heddels.com/2013/11/david-hieatt-founder-hiut-denim-exclusive-interview/.

37 Tim Walker, "Hiut: Made in Britain and Made to Last," *Independent*, March 19, 2012, https://www.independent.

co.uk/life-style/fashion/features/hiut-made-britain-and-made-last-7576601.html.

38 David Hieatt, "Love + Purpose," *Do One Thing Well* (blog), May 26, 2011, https://davidhieatt.typepad.com/doonethingwell/2011/05/love-purpose.html.

39 Jo Leevers, "Tales from Wales: Meet the Couple behind Do Lectures," *Guardian*, December 11, 2016, https://www.theguardian.com/lifeandstyle/2016/dec/11/tales-from-wales-do-lectures-howies-clare-david-hieatt.

40 Hieatt, "Love + Purpose."

41 Hieatt, "Love + Purpose."

42 Karl West, "Selvedge Job: Jeans Company Helps Welsh Town Get Back in Its Stride," *Guardian*, February 11, 2014, https://www.theguardian.com/business/2014/feb/11/selvedge-jeans-company-welsh-town.

43 Will Smale and Greg Brosnan, "How a Welsh Jeans Firm Became a Cult Global Brand," BBC, December 13, 2017, https://www.bbc.com/news/business-42237426.

44 West, "Selvedge Job."

45 Smale and Brosnan, "How a Welsh Jeans Firm."

46 Smale and Brosnan, "How a Welsh Jeans Firm."

47 Tibor Krausz, "The Red Bull Story: How World's Top Energy Drink Began in Thailand, but It Took an Austrian to Make It a Global Phenomenon," *South China Morning Post*, July 28, 2018, https://www.scmp.com

/lifestyle/food-drink/article/2156996/red-bull-story-how-worlds-top-energy-drink-began-thailand-it.

48 Tibor Krausz, "The Red Bull Story."

49 Hiut Denim, "100 days of 1% Better—Day 1, the Idea," Hiut Denim (blog), June 1, 2020, https://hiutdenim. co.uk/blogs/rivet-press/100-days-of-1-better.

Part 3: Putting Storytelling to Work for You

50 "About Us," Charity: water, last accessed June 5, 2021, https://www.charitywater.org/about.

51 Madeline Stone, "A 2004 Email from Jeff Bezos Eexplains Why PowerPoint Presentations Aren't Allowed at Amazon," *Insider*, July 28, 2015, https:// www.businessinsider.com/jeff-bezos-email-against-powerpoint-presentations-2015-7?r=US&IR=T.

52 Stone, "A 2004 Email."

53 Jeff Bezos, Letter to shareholders, 2017, https://www.sec .gov/Archives/edgar/data/1018724/000119312518121161/ d456916dex991.htm.

54 Ian McAllister, "What Is Amazon's Approach to Product Development and Product Management?" Quora, 2012, https://www.quora.com/What-is-Amazons-approach-to-product-development-and-product-management/ answer/Ian-McAllister.

55 Jack Murray and James Phelan, "Robert McKee:

Hollywood's Master Storyteller," *MediaHQ Podcast*, June 15, 2015.

56 Murray and Phelan, "Robert McKee."

57 Ira Glass, "Ira Glass on Storytelling 3," July 11, 2009, warphotography, video, 5:20, https://www.youtube.com/watch?v=X2wLP0izeJE.

58 Marriott International, "Kathleen Matthews Named Executive Vice President—Global Communications and Public Affairs for Marriott International," press release, Hospitality Net, July 11, 2006, https://www.hospitalitynet.org/news/4028132.html.

59 Bill Marriott, "A Salute to the 100th Hotel of the JW Marriott Brand," *Marriott on the Move* (blog), February 3, 2021, https://www.blogs.marriott.com/marriott-on-the-move/2021/01/a-salute-to-the-100th-hotel-of-the-jw-marriott-brand.html.

60 Freddy Mayhew, "London Council Loses Appeal to Keep Publishing £500,000-a-Year Fortnightly Freesheet," *Press Gazette*, August 8, 2019, https://www.pressgazette.co.uk/london-hackney-council-loses-appeal-to-keep-publishing-fortnightly-newspaper/.

61 Ed Sheridan, "Today in the Life? Town Hall Insists Replacement for Controversial Freesheet Contains 'Information, Not News,'" *Hackney Citizen*, July 22, 2019, https://www.hackneycitizen.co.uk/2019/07/22/hackney-life-town-hall-replacement-freesheet-information-not-news.

62 Freddy Mayhew, "Government Threatens Court Action on Town Hall 'Pravdas' in Two London Boroughs," *Press Gazette,* November 7, 2017, https://www.pressgazette.co.uk/government-threatens-court-action-on-town-hall-pravdas-in-two-london-boroughs/.

63 John Collins, "How Content Helped Intercom Grow from $1–$50M," 2018, Lean Inbound, video, 29:59, https://learninbound.com/videos/john-collins-2018/.

64 John Collins, "Why We're Dropping the Term 'Content Marketing,'" Inside Intercom, May 2, 2017, https://www.intercom.com/blog/why-were-dropping-the-term-content-marketing/.

65 Sara Yin and Stacie Pahl, "The Top Marketing Statistics for 2018 and Why They Matter," Inside Intercom, May 14, 2018, https://www.intercom.com/blog/the-top-2018-marketing-statistics-and-why-they-matter/.

66 "Intercom on Starting up," Intercom Resources, accessed June 3, 2021, https://www.intercom.com/resources/books/intercom-starting-up.

Lightning Source UK Ltd.
Milton Keynes UK
UKHW041252271121
394692UK00002B/308